OSPREY COMBAT AIRCRAFT • 46

US NAVY HORNET
UNITS OF OPERATION
IRAQI FREEDOM
PART ONE

SERIES EDITOR: TONY HOLMES

OSPREY COMBAT AIRCRAFT • 46

US NAVY HORNET UNITS OF OPERATION IRAQI FREEDOM

PART ONE

TONY HOLMES

OSPREY
PUBLISHING

Front cover
On the morning of 10 April 2003
Capt Mark Fox, Commander of
CVW-2, launched from the deck of
USS *Constellation* (CV-64) on his
12th Operation *Iraqi Freedom* sortie.
Accompanied by his wingman,
Lt Cdr Steve Cargill from VFA-137,
he held south of Baghdad in
F/A-18C BuNo 164698;

'Flying as "Minx 11", and tasked
with providing Close Air Support
(CAS), I checked in with the E-2
controller. Lt Cdr Cargill and I then
started working down a list of
frequencies in search of a Forward
Air Controller (FAC) who might need
our help. Finally, the E-2 controller
told us to go and check in with
"Diablo 69", but I couldn't raise him
on the radio. I told the E-2 that we
had no comms with "Diablo 69",
so he instructed us to head further
south, giving us the FAC's location –
85AS, Keypad 3. We then realised
that he was down in An Najaf, about
a hundred miles south of us.

'We started driving south, and the
controller informed us that our guy
on the ground was using a weak
hand-held radio, desperate for help.
This did not sound good, as we had
captured An Najaf weeks ago. We
finally checked in with our contact,
and it turned out that he was a GI
trying to distribute humanitarian aid
in the plaza outside the city's Imam
Ali Mosque. Dealing with desperate,
starving people, he was facing a near
riot. Assuring us there was no
threat, he asked us to fly a series of
high speed, low altitude passes to
distract or disperse the crowd.

'Skeptical of the FAC's "no-
threat" assessment, I was greatly
concerned about AAA or MANPADS.
Carefully scoping out the scene, and
maintaining good mutual support,
Lt Cdr Cargill and I came up with a
gameplan – we'd swap roles,
keeping one set of eyes looking for
ground fire while the other made a
high-speed flyby, always coming
from a different direction.

'We flew several passes over An
Najaf, which looked like something
out of the Bible – surrounded by
desert plains and sat amongst palm
trees on a tributary of the Euphrates
River. Seemingly untouched by
modern structures, there were lots
of single-storey, dull brown
buildings, and in the middle of them
was this huge, gold-domed mosque.

'I was looking at my gas gauge
and my watch, thinking "how much
time can I give this guy?" On my first
pass I was 100 ft above ground level
at 500 knots, just about co-altitude
with the mosque's dome. I then
rolled into a left "knife-edge", using
the dome as a "pylon", Reno air
races style, pulling about 5Gs. I
stroked the afterburner for noise as
I passed the city centre in the turn,
popping chaff and flares and moving
the jet around fairly aggressively.

'Glancing down on the plaza as
I rocked up on my wing in the turn,
a snapshot freeze-frame image of a
startled Iraqi boy looking up with his
mouth in a perfect "O" and his eyes
literally on stalks registered in my
mind. He was standing with his
mother on the corner of the square,
diagonally across from the Imam Ali
Mosque.

'I smiled to myself and breathed a
prayer: "Lord, please let that little
guy grow up to be a pilot – he'll
never forget his first up-close
glimpse of an aeroplane!"

'"Diablo 69" seemed happy with
our help, and he thanked us as we
climbed away' (*Cover artwork by
Mark Postlethwaite*)

Dedication

**This volume is dedicated to the memory of Lt Nathan 'OJ' White, killed in
action on the night of 2 April 2003**

First published in Great Britain in 2004 by Osprey Publishing
1st Floor Elms Court, Chapel Way, Botley, Oxford, OX2 9LP

ISBN 1 84176 801 4

Written & Edited by Tony Holmes
Page design by Tony Truscott
Cover Artwork by Mark Postlethwaite
Aircraft Profiles by Chris Davey
Index by Alan Thatcher
Origination by Grasmere Digital Imaging, Leeds, UK
Printed in Hong Kong through Bookbuilders

04 05 06 07 08   10 9 8 7 6 5 4 3 2 1

For a catalogue of all Osprey Publishing titles please contact us at:

Osprey Direct UK, PO Box 140, Wellingborough, Northants NN8 4ZA, UK
Email: info@ospreydirect.co.uk

Osprey Direct USA, c/o Motorbooks International, 729 Prospect Ave,
PO Box 1, Osceola, WI 54020,USA
Email: info@Ospreydirectusa.com

Or visit our website: **www.ospreypublishing.com**

CONTENTS

INTRODUCTION

Dubbed by many TACAIR insiders the 'Hornet's War', the aerial phase of Operation *Iraqi Freedom* (OIF) was indeed dominated by the US Navy's primary strike fighter, the Boeing (formerly McDonnell Douglas) F/A-18 Hornet. Proving this point, according to America's top air commander during OIF, Gen Michael Moseley, some 250 Hornets of all variants (and including 14 Royal Australian Air Force F/A-18As) were involved in the campaign. By comparison, the USAF deployed 131 F-16C/CJs and 90 F-15C/Es, which performed similar missions to the Hornet. The Royal Air Force's frontline force in-theatre consisted of 30 Tornado GR 4s, 14 Tornado F 3s and 18 Harrier GR 7s. But enough of the statistics.

This volume is the first of three in the *Combat Aircraft* series covering OIF from the Hornet community's point of view – subsequent titles will feature the Navy F/A-18 units that waged war in northern Iraq from aircraft carriers in the eastern Mediterranean and the contribution made by US Marine Corps and RAAF Hornets.

The jet enjoyed a highly successful war, being used for virtually every TACAIR mission imaginable, attacking all manner of targets spread across the length and breadth of Iraq. This book focuses on the exploits of the F/A-18 units that saw combat flying from aircraft carriers in the Northern Arabian Gulf (NAG) between 19 March and 18 April 2003, when the bulk of the OIF air war took place.

Acknowledgements

A number of the Navy pilots who saw action with the Hornet in OIF have contributed to this book, and the finished volume is much better for their input. Access to US servicemen and women who are fighting the War on Terror has tightened up considerably in the post 9/11 world that we now live in. However, thanks to the US Navy's CHINFO News Desk in the Pentagon, I was able to meet and interview key Hornet pilots soon after their arrival back in the USA from OIF. I would like to take this opportunity to thank CHINFO's Lt Cdr Danny Hernandez and Lt(jg) David Luckett for processing my request so expeditiously, and NAS Lemoore's Public Affairs Officer Dennis McGrath, who gave up the best part of a week to provide me with an on base escort.

Thank you also to my old friend and fellow naval aviation stalwart Peter Mersky, whose constructive criticism of the text and generous hospitality during my road trip were most welcome in equal measure. Thanks also to Photographer's Mate 3rd Class Todd Frantom, who supplied examples of his excellent CVW-5 OIF imagery, as did Christopher J Madden, Director Navy Visual News Service. Photographers Iwan Bogels, Dave Brown, Capt Doug Glover (of VMFA(AW)-533), Michael Groves, Gert Kromhout, Richard Siudak and Ginno Yukihisa also made important contributions, as did David Isby. Finally, thanks to the pilots and WSOs from the following units, whose OIF experiences are featured in this volume;

CVW-2 – Capt Mark Fox, Capt Craig Geron, Capt Larry Burt and Lt Cdr Zeno Rausa
CVW-11 – Capt Chuck Wright
VFA-25 – Cdr Don Braswell
VFA-41 – Lt Cdr Mark Weisgerber and Lt(jg) Josh Appezzato
VFA-87 – Cdr Greg Fenton
VFA-94 – Lt(jg) Jeff Latham
VFA-113 – Cdr Bill Dooris, Lt Cdr Paul Olin, Lt Cdr Sean Thompson and Lt Cdr Sean Williams
VFA-115 – Cdr Jeff Penfield, Cdr Dale Horan and Lt John Turner
VFA-137 – Cdr Walt Stammer
VFA-151 – Cdr Mark Hubbard, Lt Cdr Ron Candiloro, Lt Cdr Richard Thompson and Lt Cdr Kyle Weaver
VF-2 – Cdr Doug Denneny
VFA-192 – Lt John Allison

Tony Holmes, Sevenoaks, Kent, April 2004

OSW

For a generation of US Navy light strike pilots, combat operations have meant participation in Operation *Desert Storm* in 1991 and/or the enforcement of the No-Fly Zone over southern Iraq which followed in its wake. The first of these zones was created in the aftermath of *Desert Storm* in an effort to offer protection to the Kurdish population in northern Iraq from Saddam's forces. Initially established over all Iraqi territory north of the 36th parallel as part of Operation *Provide Comfort* in late 1991, the legality of this mission was mandated by United Nations Security Council Resolution 688.

When the Shi'ite Muslims also began to suffer persecution in the south, a No-Fly Zone was created with UN backing as Operation *Southern Watch* (OSW) on 26 August 1992. Joint Task Force-Southwest Asia (JTF-SWA), consisting of units from the United States, Britain, France and Saudi Arabia, was established on the same date to oversee the day-to-day running of OSW.

Like the operation in the north, which was officially titled Operation *Northern Watch* (ONW) on 1 January 1997, OSW saw US, British and French aircraft enforcing the Security Council mandate that prevented the Iraqis from flying military aircraft or helicopters below the 32nd parallel – this was increased to the 33rd parallel in September 1996. Further restrictions, including the introduction of a No-Drive Zone in the south following Iraq's hasty mobilisation and deployment of forces along the Kuwaiti border in October 1994, were introduced several years later. These were created to prevent the Iraqis from moving fixed and mobile surface-to-air missile (SAM) launchers into the southern No-Fly Zone.

The French government withdrew its support for both ONW and OSW in the late 1990s, leaving US and British air arms to continue the policing of both exclusion zones. The US Air Force and Navy, Royal Air Force and, on occasion, Fleet Air Arm became adept at monitoring what Saddam's troops were up to over much of northern and southern Iraq.

The US Navy's principal contribution to OSW was the mighty carrier battle group, controlled by Fifth Fleet (which had been formed in July

Flying from the deck of USS *Carl Vinson* (CVN-70), VFA-94 was heavily involved in the final night strikes of Operation *Desert Fox* on 19 December 1998. This four-day campaign saw numerous targets hit across southern Iraq, including a presidential palace at Lake Tharthar, just south of Baghdad. In the aftermath of *Desert Fox*, CVN-70 completed the longest combat line period for a carrier since the Vietnam War, and the vessel's CVW-11 also expended further ordnance during the course of innumerable OSW patrols that continued into late March 1999. This photograph of VFA-94's 'Hobo 410' (BuNo 164048) was taken in early 1999 in the NAG, the jet configured for the DCA role with two underwing AIM-120A AMRAAMs and two wingtip-mounted AIM-9L Sidewinders. Delivered to the Navy in July 1990, BuNo 164048 has served exclusively with VFA-94. During its 14 years of service with the 'Mighty Shrikes', the Hornet has flown numerous OSW patrols and seen combat in *Desert Fox*, OEF and OIF. In the latter campaigns it was the squadron's 'CAG jet', marked up as 'Hobo 400' – see the photograph on page 78 (*VFA-94*)

1995) as part of the unified US Central Command (CENTCOM), which oversaw operations in the region. Typically, an aircraft carrier would be on station in the Northern Arabian Gulf (NAG) at all times, vessels spending around three to four months of a standard six-month deployment committed to OSW. Ships from both the Atlantic and Pacific fleets took it in turns to 'stand the watch', sharing the policing duties in the No-Fly Zone with USAF and RAF assets ashore at bases in Saudi Arabia, Kuwait, Oman and other allied countries in the region.

OSW's original brief was to deter the repression of the Kurdish and Shi'ite populations and impose a No-Fly Zone, but it soon became obvious to the Coalition that the Iraqi Army was more than capable of dealing with the disruptive elements in both the north and the south without having to involve the Air Force. Frustrated by its inability to defend the people it had encouraged to rise up and overthrow Saddam's regime in 1991, the US-led Coalition subtly changed the emphasis of its ONW and OSW mission. This saw the systematic monitoring of Iraqi military activity in the area evolve from being a useful secondary mission tasking to the primary role of the crews conducting these sorties from the mid 1990s. By December 1998, the justification put forward by the US government for the continuation of both ONW and OSW was the protection of Iraq's neighbours from any potential aggression, and to ensure the admission, and safety, of UN weapons inspectors.

Most OSW missions were mundane and boring according to the naval aircrew who had flown them. However, this all changed with the implementation of Operation *Desert Fox* on 16 December 1998, which saw the launching of a four-day aerial offensive ostensibly aimed at curbing Iraq's ability to produce Weapons of Mass Destruction (WMD). Although triggered by Saddam's unwillingness to cooperate with UN inspections of weapons sites, many observers believed that the primary aim of *Desert Fox* was to attack the Iraqi leadership in a series of decapitation strikes. To this end, a presidential palace south of Baghdad was hit, as were buildings housing the Special Security Organisation and the Special Republican Guard.

The carriers USS *Enterprise* (CVN-65) and USS *Carl Vinson* (CVN-70) played a key role in *Desert Fox*, the vessels' CVW-3 and CVW-11 flying more than 400 sorties in the 25+ strikes launched during the campaign.

Although *Desert Fox* lasted just a matter of days, its consequences were felt right up until OIF in

Having completed yet another uneventful patrol over southern Iraq, the pilot of Lot XII F/A-18C 'Hobo 410' returns to the marshall overhead CVN-70. His jet is carrying a single 500-lb GBU-12 Paveway II LGB on its outer wing pylon, this weapon having proved its worth time and time again during *Desert Fox*. Aside from dropping a number of LGBs during its 1998-99 cruise, VFA-94 (along with sister-squadron VFA-22) also gave the revolutionary AGM-154A JSOW its combat debut on 25 January 1999 when it knocked out an SA-3 SAM complex near Basra. This particular site had plagued Coalition aircraft since the end of *Desert Storm* due to its position at a key choke point in southern Iraq (*VFA-94*)

VFA-37, embarked on the USS *Enterprise* (CVN-65), also made history during *Desert Fox* when it sent female TACAIR pilots into combat for the very first time. Back from their mission on 17 December 1998, two naval aviators conduct a traditional fighter pilot's debrief in the VFA-37 ready room (*US Navy*)

March 2003. Proclaiming a victory after UN weapons inspectors had left Iraq on the eve of the bombing campaign, Saddam brazenly challenged patrolling ONW and OSW aircraft by moving mobile SAM batteries and AAA weapons into the exclusion zones. Both were used in the coming months, and Iraqi combat aircraft also started to push more regularly into the No-Fly Zones.

In the post-*Desert Fox* world, these violations provoked a swift, but measured, response from JTF-SWA's Combined Air Operations Center (CAOC), which controlled the entire No-Fly Zone mission planning element, and created a daily Air Tasking Order (ATO) for all Coalition participants (both naval and shore-based aviation assets). Typically, such missions were devised within the CAOC-approved pre-planned retaliatory strike framework, and they soon became known as Response Options (ROs). The latter allowed No-Fly Zone enforcers to react to threats or incursions in a coordinated manner through the execution of agreed ROs against pre-determined targets such as SAM and AAA sites and command and control nodes.

The level of conflict in the southern region remained high into the new millennium, and between March 2000 and March 2001, Coalition aircraft were engaged more than 500 times by SAMs and AAA while flying 10,000 sorties into Iraqi airspace. In response to this aggression, which had seen Coalition aircraft fired on 60 times since 1 January 2001, US and British jets dropped bombs on 38 occasions. The most comprehensive of these RO strikes (the biggest since *Desert Fox*) occurred on 16 February 2001 when CVW-3, aboard the USS *Harry S Truman* (CVN-75), hit five command, control and communications sites.

The steady escalation of the conflict in the region was only brought to a halt, albeit temporarily, by the devastating attacks on the World Trade Center and the Pentagon on 11 September 2001. The subsequent declaration of the War on Terror by President George W Bush saw carrier battle groups under Fifth Fleet control removed from their OSW station and sent east into the Arabian Sea and Indian Ocean in support of Operation *Enduring Freedom* (OEF) in Afghanistan.

With the bulk of the tactical airpower in this conflict provided by carrier aircraft flying arduous eight- to ten-hour missions over land-locked Afghanistan, OSW No-Fly Zone operations by the US

'Ordies' from VFA-94 wheel an Aero-12C weapons skid, laden down with a 2000-lb GBU-10 Paveway II LGB, along the flight deck of CVN-70 in January 1999 (*VFA-94*)

CVW-17, embarked in the USS *George Washington* (CVN-73), conducted the Navy's first OSW missions in almost a year after entering the NAG in early September 2002. On the 5th of that month four F/A-18Cs attacked Al Rutbah South air base, some 240 miles due west of Baghdad. Several more RO strikes were conducted over the next three weeks prior to CVN-73 departing the NAG on 20 September and heading into the Mediterranean. CVW-17 boasted three Navy-manned F/A-18C units, namely VFA-34, VFA-81 and VFA-83. All three got to drop ordnance during CVN-73's brief spell in the NAG (*Capt Dana Potts/US Navy*)

Navy were drastically scaled back. This allowed the Iraqis to move more air defence weaponry below the 32nd parallel.

By the spring of 2002 the Taliban regime had been removed from power in Afghanistan, and the US government's focus of attention returned once again to its old foe in the region, Saddam Hussein. Proof of this came with the arrival of USS *George Washington* (CVN-73), and its embarked CVW-17, in the NAG in early September 2002, the vessel's subsequent assignment to OSW marking the first time a carrier battle group had performed this mission in almost a year. Within days of its arrival on station, the air wing was conducting RO strikes after being engaged by AAA and SAM radars during patrols over southern Iraq.

Having already spent two months conducting OEF missions over Afghanistan, CVW-17's spell in the NAG was to last only three weeks. CVN-73 then headed back up into the Mediterranean Sea, and Sixth Fleet control, before returning home in December. By then its place in the NAG had been taken by the USS *Abraham Lincoln* (CVN-72), which was in the early stages of a marathon ten-and-a-half-month cruise. Like CVN-73, the vessel had supported OEF prior to its push into the NAG in late October 2002, although the aircrew of the embarked CVW-14 had not seen action during their patrols over Afghanistan. This was all set to change once they commenced OSW.

AGGRESSIVE OSW

While the tactical jets of CVW-14 continued to bore holes in the sky over Afghanistan, in Washington, D.C. the case for war against Iraq was gaining momentum as discussions about the country's alleged development and stockpiling of weapons of mass destruction (WMD) reached fever pitch. Links between Saddam's regime and Osama Bin Laden's al-Qaeda network were also played up by the Bush administration, and the end product of all this talk was the decision, in September 2002, by US Defence Secretary Donald Rumsfeld to step up the level of response to Iraqi threats to Coalition aircraft conducting OSW missions.

By the time CVN-72 flew its first No-Fly Zone patrol on 29 October, the revised ROs were well and truly in place in the CAOC. The latter had

Fresh from conducting OEF patrols over Afghanistan, USS *Abraham Lincoln* (CVN-72) steamed into the NAG from the Northern Arabian Sea in late October 2002. The vessel had been performing the OSW mission for just a matter of days when this photograph was taken in early November 2002. CVN-72 would subsequently become an almost permanent fixture in the NAG, conducting a ten-month-long extended cruise that started on 20 July 2002 and finished on 6 May 2003. For much of this time the vessel was assigned to the Fifth Fleet, either in the NAG or in the Northern Arabian Sea (*US Navy*)

moved in 2001 from military quarters in Riyadh to Prince Sultan Air Base (known as 'PSAB' to all Coalition crews), also in Saudi Arabia, thus centralising the entire OSW mission-planning element.

The man in charge of overseeing CVW-14's enforcement of the new OSW ROs was air wing commander Capt Kevin Albright, who told visiting journalists aboard CVN-72 in November 2002 that within days of arriving in the NAG he had noted a change in the way the Iraqis were opposing the Navy's operations;

'They are shooting a lot at us, and they are really trying hard to down our aircraft – not just firing up in the air. They are firing at our people.'

Albright also spoke about how the ROs being actioned in-theatre had altered significantly as well;

'We are now going after more substantive targets than two years ago. For me, dropping bombs on a command bunker is always more significant than knocking out an S-60 anti-aircraft gun'.

The first RO undertaken by CVW-14 saw two SAM launchers at Al Kut and an air defence command and control bunker at Tallil air base attacked on 6 November 2002. This mission was doubly significant, as it was the first strike conducted by aircraft from CVN-72 on the deployment, and it marked the combat debut of the F/A-18E Super Hornet. One of the pilots involved in the first successful strike by the Navy's newest tactical fighter was VFA-115's Lt John Turner, who recalled;

'My wingman and I were flying a standard day mission over southern Iraq when a section of USAF jets that had just dropped bombs on a target in response to a No-Fly Zone violation was shot at. We were on the point of returning to the tanker for gas, having been on our Vul (period of vulnerability) station for 80 minutes, when we were given clearance to conduct an immediate retaliation strike on an air defence bunker that CAOC believed was controlling some of the AAA sites in the area where the violation had occurred.

'Despite our long time on station, we still had sufficient fuel left to make the 80-mile run to the target. My wingman and I dropped our JDAM (Joint Direct Attack Munition) on the bunker, and although we were fired at, our egress was uneventful and we recovered back aboard the ship. We recorded our own BHA (Battle Hit Assessment) pictures of the drop on our standard NITE Hawk FLIR pods.'

VFA-115's Lt John Turner is greeted by CVW-14's 'ordies' upon his return to CVN-72 after dropping the air wing's first bombs of the deployment during the afternoon of 6 November 2002. He and his wingman had just attacked two SAM launchers at Al Kut and an air defence command and control bunker at Tallil air base with GBU-31(V)2/B 2000-lb JDAM. This mission marked the combat debut of the Super Hornet, Lt Turner flying F/A-18E BuNo 165783 and his wingman BuNo 165787 (*Lt John Turner*)

Lt Turner gives a thumb's up to the deck crew on CVN-72 prior to climbing out of his Super Hornet on the evening of 6 November 2002 (*Lt John Turner*)

Lt Turner (right) congratulates his wingman in the wake of the first Super Hornet bomb-drop. Note that both pilots have no squadron patches or name tags on their desert tan flightsuits (*Lt John Turner*)

A VFA-25 F/A-18C is readied for its next OSW patrol aboard CVN-72 in November 2002, the aircraft carrying a single GBU-31(V)2/B 2000-lb JDAM under each wing. In the foreground are finless AIM-120C AMRAAMs, one of which will be uploaded onto the Hornet in this photograph. The guidance fins are fitted to the missile after it has been attached to the fuselage (or wing) weapon station (*US Navy*)

The importance of this mission to the Navy as a whole, and CVW-14 in particular, was brought home to Lt Turner upon his return to the ship;

'The first thing you do when you get back to the carrier after dropping weapons is turn your mission tapes in and get them reviewed and verified for the accuracy of your bombing. Normally, it is just you and the squadron intelligence officer who review the tapes, but on this occasion by the time I walked into the squadron ready room the CTF-50 admiral, the captain of the ship, CAG Albright and my boss were all standing there waiting anxiously to see the video! These guys were more interested in the fact that it was the first time that CVW-14 had dropped bombs in OSW on this cruise, rather than the first time the Super Hornet had expended ordnance in anger. Fortunately for my wingman and I, the video showed four perfect hits! With JDAM, you plug in your coordinates, and as long as they are accurate the bomb is going to hit the target. The weapon makes BHA and collateral damage assessment very easy.'

VFA-115 conducted further strikes the following day and on 10 November, as JTF/SWA's new approach to OSW gained momentum.

RO EVOLUTION

It is appropriate at this juncture to backtrack a little bit and see how the ROs carried out by CVW-14 in the lead up to OIF were formulated by JTF/SWA. The adoption of response options as the primary means of enforcing the OSW/ONW mission evolved to match the Coalition's desire to ensure the safety of its crews flying over Iraqi territory. Initially, the near-immediate air strike response to SAFIREs (surface-to-air fires, involving AAA or SAMs) that had been the norm before and immediately after Operation *Desert Fox* was replaced with delayed, punitive strikes that were usually flown the same day as the No-Fly Zone violation took place.

This RO evolved post-9/11 into an even more considered approach, whereby the Coalition adopted the policy of attacking any Iraqi military target in the southern No-Fly Zone. It did not even have to be the one that prompted the reaction in the first place. This, in turn, led to the adoption of the pre-planned RO methodology in the final months of OSW, as the battlefield for OIF was prepped.

The Hornet had been at the heart of the Navy's OSW commitment right from the start, following on from its participation in *Desert Storm*. In the decade that No-Fly Zone missions were flown over southern Iraq, the bulk of these sorties were performed by light strike units from both the Pacific and Atlantic Fleets, as well as the Marine Corps.

The aircraft also evolved in that time from being essentially a fair weather fighter-bomber that relied primarily on 'dumb' bombs to destroy its targets, to a sophisticated all-weather strike platform capable of servicing a multitude of DMPIs (Designated Mean Point of Impact) in a single mission with GPS- and laser-guided weapons. The Hornet's

effectiveness as an air superiority fighter has also been improved against the backdrop of OSW following the introduction of the AIM-120 AMRAAM missile in the late 1990s. Finally, the jet's 'killer' role in the crucial Suppression of Enemy Air Defences (SEAD) mission has been honed to an unprecedented level through the regular employment of the AGM-88 High-speed Anti-Radiation Missile (HARM) and the Joint Stand-Off Weapon (JSOW) against AAA and SAM sites in OSW.

The actual 'nuts and bolts' of a typical No-Fly Zone mission did not alter hugely during the latter years of OSW, with most following a set pattern as follows. Thanks to the established routine of the operation, and the advent of secure e-mail communication between the CAOC and the air wing aboard the carrier in the NAG, shipboard mission planners usually got a rough outline of the ATO 'frag' (tasking) about 72 hours before it was due to be flown. As each day passed, more information would be relayed to the ship to the point where, 24 hours before the package was due to launch, its participants had a detailed plan of where they were going and what they were doing, as well as the role being played by other supporting assets participating from shore bases.

On the day of the mission, assigned crews would start their OSW briefing about two-and-half hours prior to launching. This was an air wing-wide meeting that was usually attended by all aircrew participating in the mission. This lasted for around 30 to 45 minutes, after which crews would return to their own squadron ready rooms and conduct the division brief applicable to their part of the mission – this ran for about 15 minutes. Hornet crews then broke up into sections and conducted individual briefs, where they would discuss things like in-flight emergencies, and what to do during the sortie from a single aircraft standpoint. This process would effectively see the participating units go from 'back row' to 'mid-level' to 'micro view'.

One of the air wing's biggest advantages when compared with shore-based OSW assets was that all mission elements briefed together, face-to-face. Air wings would do this nearly every day on cruise, talking at length about various mission profiles and operational developments. This also allowed the Navy to run bigger packages into Iraq. USAF groups, on the other hand, all briefed separately and then met up to support each other inbound to the 'Box', as southern Iraq was dubbed by US aircrews.

Although employed primarily as a 'bomb truck', the Hornet can also perform both the DCA and SEAD missions quite effectively. Configured for the latter role is VFA-25's 'Fist 406' (BuNo 164654), which has an AGM-88 HARM attached to its starboard outer pylon. The unit fired a number of HARM rounds both in OSW and OIF. Emphasising the DCA aspect of the Hornet's multi-role capabilities, the VFA-113 jet (BuNo 164682) being stroked along waist cat three is carrying an AIM-7M Sparrow III on an LAU-115 launcher, attached to the jet's outer wing pylon (*US Navy*)

A Hornet pilot from VFA-113 conducts a preflight, deck-level walkaround of his jet prior to heading for southern Iraq (*US Navy*)

VFA-113's 'Sting 302' (BuNo 164648) tops off its tanks over the NAG prior to pressing into southern Iraq on 7 November 2002. CVW-14 expended more ordnance on this date following further violations of the No-Fly Zone. The Hornet is receiving fuel from a 6th Air Refueling Squadron (ARS)/60th Air Mobility Wing (AMW) KC-10A, flying out of Al Dhafra air base in the United Arab Emirates. Typically, Navy OSW packages would 'hit' a 'big wing' tanker just prior to pushing into Iraq, and then get more fuel after completing their Vul time in the 'Box' (*US Navy*)

Toting a pair of AIM-120C AMRAAMs and wingtip-mounted AIM-9Ms, 'Sting 306' (BuNo 164634) cruises over the cloud-covered NAG in November 2002. Most OSW sorties took the form of uneventful DCA patrols, with Hornets typically flying in this configuration (*Lt Cdr Sean Williams*)

Hornet pilots would go 'feet on the deck' to their jets 45 minutes prior to launching, by which time the aircraft was fully fuelled, all systems (bar the engines) were up and running thanks to the jet's auxiliary power unit and the pylon-mounted weapons had been secured.

The F/A-18 was then preflighted at deck level for around 10-15 minutes, after which the pilot climbed aboard. With 30 minutes to run to launch, the air wing's Air Boss (who runs the flight deck) would call 'starts away', and the aircraft were fired up. With everything functioning as it should be, the Hornets would be unchained and marshalled in a pre-ordained order to one of the ship's four catapults for launching.

Having successfully departed the carrier, the pilot would find the duty tanker using the Hornet's APG-73 radar in air-to-air search mode, rather than 'breaking comms' in order to get a steer from an AWACS controller. Having located the tanker, he would join the line of aircraft formating off its left wing, waiting his turn to cycle through and 'top off' the Hornet's tanks. With the refuelling complete, the pilot positioned himself back in the formation, but this time off the tanker's right wing.

Most strike groups were then divided into two mini packages once on station so as to cover any periods of vulnerability – this tasking was easier to perform when dealing with smaller gaggles of aircraft, rather than sending in a huge formation of jets that just tended to get in each others' way. The first group would commence its Vul time, leaving the second package on station for a short while longer prior to it too being committed. There was a brief period of overlap between the two packages as a result of this tactic being employed.

Each package had a designated Vul time in the 'Box' according to the ATO, and each of these time slots had been meticulously worked out by CAOC. It was standard operational procedure that if the package did not make it into Iraq between its time slots, the jets would not be allowed 'over the beach'.

Once in the 'Box', the aircraft pressed on along pre-planned routes until arriving on their designated patrol station in south-eastern Iraq. Crews remained in constant contact with one of four Air Traffic Control agencies while on an OSW mission, one of which was on a US Navy ship in the NAG, another on land near the Iraqi border, a third in the 'big wing' USAF or RAF tanker that was on station to refuel the package and the fourth in an orbiting E-2 or E-3 AWACS platform. These platforms kept all TACAIR elements in Iraq updated on what was happening in response to the mission.

As previously mentioned, towards the end of OSW CAOC instigated a more aggressive RO regime that regularly saw the issuing of ATOs which called for a measured response to increasing Iraqi violations of the No-Fly Zone. In such cases the air wing worked up a strike profile for both the CAOC-chosen target and a secondary target, after which it would launch its aircraft in exactly the same manner as detailed above. Alternately, as was the case with the first CVW-14 strike of its final OSW cruise, CAOC could call for an RO to be executed while a package was in flight if a serious misdemeanour had been perpetrated by the Iraqis.

With the mission completed, the package would go 'feet wet' back over the NAG and head along pre-planned routes south to a tanker – either a 'big winged' USAF KC-10 or KC-135, a RAF VC10 or Tristar or two 'organic' S-3 Vikings sortied with the strike package from the carrier. Cycling through the refuelling procedure once again, topping off their tanks at about 500 lbs above what was needed to land back aboard the ship, the aircraft would overfly the carrier, proceed back into marshal and then await their turn to recover. A typical OSW mission usually lasted around four hours, depending on whether an RO was prosecuted during the course of the sortie.

CVW-2 ENTERS THE FRAY

On 17 December 2002 CVN-72 was relieved of its OSW tasking by the USS *Constellation* (CV-64), performing its 21st, and last, operational deployment in its 41st year of service with the US Navy. Embarked

Aside from 'big wing' tankers, the Navy's fleet of elderly S-3B Vikings provided much needed organic refuelling support for TACAIR assets on virtually every OSW flight. Seen here giving 'gas' to a thirsty Hornet from VFA-151, this particular VS-38 Viking was lost over the side of the *Constellation* at 0510 hrs on 1 April 2003. Having landed safely following a routine tanking flight, the jet lost nosewheel steering and brakes due to a hydraulic failure/leak of some sort while taxiing on a wet deck and ran off the side of the ship into the safety netting. Pilot Lt Ben Folkers and co-pilot Lt Matt Wilder ejected into the water at this point, and both were rescued by the HS-2 HH-60H SAR helicopter. Breaking through the netting, the S-3B hit the water and sunk to a depth of 200 ft. It was not recovered (*VFA-151*)

USS *Constellation* (CV-64) arrived in the NAG on 17 December 2002, having set sail from its home port of NAS North Island, California, on 2 November 2002 (*US Navy*)

aboard the vessel for its 'Sunset Cruise' were the 72 aircraft of CVW-2. 'Connie' and its air wing were seasoned OSW campaigners, having jointly enforced the No-Fly Zone on their previous four cruises between 1995 and 2001. In that time CVW-2 had racked up an impressive 50 weeks of OSW flying, its units having flown 5000+ sorties policing the No-Fly Zone.

The air wing undertook its first mission into Iraq on 19 December 2002, and Hornets struck targets as part of an RO the following day. One of the pilots involved in the latter strike was Lt Cdr Ron Candiloro of VFA-151;

'Some 90 per cent of the squadron's OSW flying pre-war saw us manning CAPs over Iraq in conjunction with the deployed USAF F-15Cs flying out of Saudi Arabia. Every once in a while we would get to perform an RO strike if the senior officers in "PSAB" decided that the Iraqis were getting too close to our patrolling aircraft with their AAA. I was involved in the first real time mission of the deployment, which saw CVW-2 conduct an RO as a result of AAA activity. The USAF had an RQ-1 Predator UAV flying over southern Iraq at the time, CENTCOM testing its ability to find a target, send its video imagery back to "PSAB" via an AWACS, have the analysts mensurate the target coordinates and then get these relayed directly out to a TACAIR platform on station that had GPS weaponry capability. The jets were then instructed to hit the target. I actually got to drop the first GPS bombs delivered on a target located by a Predator in OSW.

'The UAV had located a AAA piece, and within 15 minutes of the imagery having been taken, "PSAB" was relaying coordinates to me via an E-2. I was already on station flying over a kill box with my wingman when we were given the attack coordinates by our controller via Strike Con – one of our secure frequencies. I typed in the coordinates, headed to the target and dropped my JDAM directly onto the AAA site. Very few time-sensitive response options were conducted after this mission, and I think that my strike in conjunction with the UAV was the only one that CVW-2 flew prior to OIF.'

Commenting on this first air wing strike, Commander of CVW-2, Capt Mark Fox, remarked;

'It immediately became clear we would not repeat last deployment's "Groundhog Day" pattern. Conducting a Response Option attack on only our third day of operations in the Gulf, we had destroyed several different Iraqi targets and delivered more ordnance and hit more aim points in one strike than we had during the entire 2001 deployment.'

On 22 December a Predator UAV was shot down by an Iraqi Air Force MiG-25 and AAA while flying in the vicinity of Kut, 100 miles south-east of Baghdad. The fourth drone to be downed by the Iraqis during OSW (three had been destroyed in August, September and October 2001), its

JDAM was CAOC's preferred weapon of choice in the final months of OSW following several wayward LGB strikes by both Navy and USAF TACAIR assets in the autumn of 2002. Reflecting the prevailing J-weapon mindset, VFA-137 have armed this Hornet with a single 1000-lb GBU-35(V)1/B JDAM on each outer wing pylon. The jet also carries two AIM-9Ms and a single AIM-120C AMRAAM for self-defence, as well as its 20 mm M61A1 Vulcan cannon. Like its sister Hornet squadrons within CVW-2, VFA-137 saw plenty of action in the final weeks of OSW, as unit CO Cdr Walt Stammer explains;

'In the lead up to OIF, I could tell that CENTCOM was authorising far more Response Options than had previously been the case on OSW deployments – this was most obvious when you were airborne on patrol, as there seemed to be plenty of ROs being performed all over southern Iraq. Having said that, the Iraqis were much keener to oppose our patrols with AAA the closer we got to the war.

'Typically, the ROs were flown on the same day that the Coalition aircraft had been fired on, and in some cases bombs were dropped during the very same mission. The threat level posed by the Iraqi ground forces dictated how quickly the RO was actioned.

'We got to conduct RO strikes on radars sited on airfields, as well as attacking Republican Guard barracks in western Iraq. We used JDAM on all these missions, and were opposed by AAA' (*VFA-137*)

Assembled and ready for loading, 1000-lb GBU-35(V)1/B JDAM crowd the hangar bay of CV-64 on the eve of OIF. All of these weapons would be carefully wheeled onto one of the ship's four elevators and then taken up to the flight deck en masse. Once 'up on the roof', the ordnance would be collected by teams of armourers from the various Hornet and Tomcat squadrons, who would take the bombs away for loading onto their jets (*US Navy*)

loss provoked a measured response from CAOC on 26 December, as explained by Capt Fox. Flying one of 12 F/A-18C strikers covered by two F-14Ds performing the defensive counter air role and an EA-6B servicing the electronic warfare aspect of the mission, Fox was dropping bombs in anger for the first time since *Desert Storm* in February 1991;

'I led the response option strike following the Predator incident. The RO that we flew was not a "tit-for-tat" response, however, and I was glad to see that JTF-SWA had moved away from such a mindset. This seemed to have been the case when CVW-2 was last in the NAG in 2001, when a "they shoot at us so we go after an S-60 AAA piece" policy apparently held sway in OSW.

'I dropped J-weapons for the first time on the 26 December mission, releasing three JDAM through a solid overcast against targets near An Nasiriyah. This mission was a perfect example of the significant change in OSW between one deployment and the next. We had JDAM capability in 2001, but we were not called upon to employ it. Things were vastly different in 2002.

'This time, I could see that we were actually attacking targets that would possibly help us in the long term should we decide to invade Iraq. Such OSW strikes included bombing cable repeaters in the south, thus preventing the Iraqi high command in Baghdad from communicating with their subordinates in Basra, and destroying command and control nodes. These targets were far more relevant to the overall conduct of any future war than blowing up a solitary S-60 hidden under a palm tree in the middle of the desert.

'Although I was not aware of any deliberate policy on JTF-SWA's behalf to prep the battlefield a full three months before OIF started, it was clear that some thought had gone into the targets that we were being asked to bomb.'

Anticipating that CVW-2 would have to 'hit the ground running' once CV-64 arrived in the NAG, Capt Fox had done his best to lay the groundwork for a hassle-free turnover with CVW-14 by sending an advanced party to liaise with CAOC in early December 2002;

'Seamless connectivity in our turnover with CVW-14 was essential, and I wanted to have absolute certainty that we understood how to operate, communicate and effectively function in the theatre. Having seen firsthand the difficulties of connecting with CAOC during Operations *Desert Shield/Storm*, as well as various contingency operations in the mid-1990s in both the Adriatic Sea and Persian Gulf, I kept a rotating team of CVW-2 liaison officers in "PSAB" to ensure that air wing-CAOC communications were strong. It was essential that planners – both afloat and ashore – fully understood how to make the tasking process work, and therefore get the most out of the air wing.

'We felt conflict was imminent upon our arrival, and kept that sense of urgency throughout our entire time – four months – in the Gulf. Every moment to plan and prepare for combat was golden. Flying almost daily over Iraq in support of OSW further prepared us for the OIF campaign. Knowing Iraq's geography, understanding the threat and carrying and expending live GPS-guided ordnance against real targets unquestionably enhanced our effectiveness once fully-blown combat began.'

The Iraqi response to the heightened OSW activity was predictable, and following the 8 November 2002 UN Security Council resolution demanding unfettered access for its inspectors to search for WMD in Iraq, Coalition jets were fired at 32 times up to the downing of the UAV.

A CVW-2 pilot involved in these final OSW missions described them as being 'very procedural, with the lawyers right there alongside CENTCOM's commanding general to ensure that we did the right thing at every turn – no freelancing of any sort by anybody.

'The name of the game was DCA (Defensive Counter-Air) in support of the ISR (Intelligence, Surveillance and Reconnaissance) assets such as Predator drones and U-2s as they gathered intel and prepped the battlefield in southern Iraq – ROs were considered secondary to all other flying operations at the time.

'A typical OSW sortie saw us launch with our weapons, refuel from USAF tankers, check in with a myriad of control agencies, do a roll call at the beginning of a Vul window and then press out and do either a Strike FAM, HARM or DCA mission. We usually flew back to southern Kuwait to get mid cycle gas. Almost all of these missions were flown at night, wearing night vision goggles (NVGs). Sometimes, an RO would be called away by CAOC at "PSAB". Routinely, the AWACS would call out the call-signs of the guys they wanted to be droppers and then switch them up another frequency. They would then send the rest back home. The Hornets were doing great work with the JDAMs at this point. It was nice to see "your strike" get the job done, especially after the hours and hours put into mission planning.'

The Strike FAM mission mentioned above proved popular in OSW. A flight would be assigned a target inside Iraq, its jets loaded with ordnance and sent to fly the strike mission, but no weapons would be employed. Such sorties allowed crews to continue providing an aerial

Having conducted yet another leaflet-dropping mission over southern Iraq, VFA-151's CO, Cdr Mark Hubbard, returns to his ship in his designated aircraft on 4 February 2003. CVW-2's TACAIR jets were amongst the most weathered naval aircraft to see combat in OIF thanks to a shortage of fresh water aboard CV-64 in early 2003. This effectively meant that deck crews were unable to wash their aircraft for extended periods – sometimes weeks on end – hence the war-like finish of 'Switch 301' (Lot XV F/A-18C BuNo 164703) *prior* to OIF commencing! Delivered to the Navy in December 1992 and immediately allocated to VFA-151, this machine was one of twelve brand new night vision-capable Lot XV jets issued to the unit in 1992-93 as replacements for the 'Vigilantes'' veteran Lot VIII F/A-18As (*VFA-151*)

Cdr Mark Hubbard poses for a self-portrait with his wingman during their flight back to the 'Connie' following a leaflet drop over southern Iraq (*VFA-151*)

Leaflets giving the frequency of the Coalition's Arabic-speaking radio station are carefully packed into the metal rings of a Psychological Dispersal Unit (PDU) aboard CV-64. CVW-2's Hornet units dropped 121 PDUs in OSW (*US Navy*)

presence in the No-Fly Zones, while at the same time familiarising (hence the FAM abbreviation in the mission designator) them with target areas, threat emitters and communications unique to the Iraqi theatre. Additionally, Strike FAMs presented crews with the opportunity to practise weapon delivery tactics and parameters in an environment closer to what they would expect to see if hostilities started.

All three Hornet units aboard CV-64 were kept busy flying Strike FAMs and prosecuting ROs in the months prior to OIF, and none more so than VFA-151 'Vigilantes', led by Cdr Mark Hubbard. Here, he recalls some of the missions flown by his squadron in the build up to war;

'In the final weeks of OSW we started to hit command and control nodes and radar relay stations in southern Iraq, as well as the many fibre optic cable repeater "vaults" that linked the south with Baghdad. These took the form of small concrete structures buried just below the ground, and they followed lines of communication such as roads and highways. The "vaults" were not visible from the air, but we could usually see the mound of dirt that ran out to them from the road. At the end of the mound would be a manhole-sized concrete cover, and below it was the housing for the repeater equipment. We hit strategically placed stations with GPS weapons in an effort to remove Saddam's ability to command and control. This would force his troops to communicate via more conventional – and jammable – means such as radios and cellular phones.

'We were being opposed by Iraqi AAA on virtually every flight that we conducted in OSW from the moment we relieved the *Lincoln* in mid-December 2002 – things just got progressively hotter over southern Iraq.

'Aside from JDAM, I also got to drop plenty of information leaflets in January and February 2003, these instructing the Iraqis not to fire at Coalition aircraft, and explaining that we were not targeting their homes, amongst other things. The leaflets also urged Iraqi commanders not to use WMD, and for frontline troops to desert, as well as illustrating the overwhelming firepower the Coalition could bring to bear – the B-52 featured a lot in these leaflets!

'We could fit 15,000 of them, rolled up like toilet paper, into an empty Rockeye pod – designated a Psychological Dispersal Unit – and you would drop two or three pods per sortie from each jet. The Hornet units in CVW-2 must have dropped close to two million of those leaflets, all of which were printed aboard the ship. The official post-war statistics reveal that 31.8 million leaflets were expended by all Coalition forces, and VFA-151 certainly delivered its fair share of them! Aside from the Hornets, the USAF also dropped leaflets from C-130s, A-10s, B-52s and F-16s.

'We would sortie as a division of four jets into southern Iraq and drop around 180,000 leaflets at a time. We let the pods go from 35,000 ft on

VFA-137's 'Falcon 404' (Lot XV F/A-18C BuNo 164709) heads for southern Iraq toting a single PDU-5/B Psychological Dispersal Unit beneath each wing. Packed with thousands of leaflets, the PDUs were dropped from a height of 35,000 ft over towns and cities in the lead up to OIF. The dispensers were simply Mk 20 Mod 3 Rockeye II cluster bomb units that had had their 247 Mk 118 Mod 0 bomblets replaced by rolls of propaganda leaflets. The yellow band on the PDU indicates the location of the charge that breaks the unit open in flight and the blue band denotes that the canister's contents are non-explosive. 'Falcon 404' also carries a 'heater' on each wingtip rail and a solitary AIM-120C round on the starboard fuselage weapon station. This aircraft was delivered new to VFA-137 in February 1993 when the unit replaced its Lot VIII F/A-18As (*VFA-137*)

'Sting 302' (BuNo 164648) carries a 500-lb LGB on its outer starboard pylon (*Lt Cdr Sean Williams*)

the outskirts of the big towns in the south, and at a pre-determined height based on the estimates of where the best wind currents were, they would open up and the leaflets would be blown over the target area.

'By using the wind, we could avoid any significant AAA or SAM threats, as the Iraqis had mobile SA-3s and Rolands in the areas where we were flying leaflet missions pre-war.

'Such sorties proved an effective way to get the Coalition message across, as few Iraqis had radios and even fewer had televisions, so information such as was printed on the leaflets would travel by word-of-mouth. Children also collected them and traded them like baseball cards!'

The leaflet-dropping missions flown by the Hornets pre-war were just a part of the overall 'psyops' campaign waged by the Coalition both before and during OIF. Although it is always difficult to quantify the success of such sorties, Fifth Fleet commander Vice Adm Timothy Keating said on 12 April 2003 that the Iraqis' reluctance to launch Scud surface-to-surface ballistic missiles during the war may have been directly attributable to this aspect of the campaign.

THE *LINCOLN* RETURNS

Having chopped out of the NAG in early December and then got as far east as Perth, Western Australia, on its way home, the *Lincoln* battle group was instructed to turn around and head back to the NAG to help bolster the Coalition forces massing in the region. The vessel returned to Perth in early January 2003 (having already spent Christmas in Western Australia) for a two-week spell of flightdeck resurfacing at anchor off Fremantle.

CVW-14 took this opportunity to put 20 aircraft ashore to conduct crew continuation training at RAAF base Pearce, before flying them back aboard ship (minus an F/A-18C from VFA-25 which ran off the runway and was damaged) when the carrier weighed anchor and headed directly to the NAG on 20 January.

The carrier was back on station by early February, and CVW-14 picked up the OSW 'ball' where it had left off some two months earlier. Some things had changed since the carrier had been away, however, as VFA-113's Lt Cdr Paul Olin explained;

'Our two periods in OSW contrasted most markedly in terms of the increased procedures that had been brought in to cope with the many more military aircraft now flying in the congested airspace of the NAG as we began the run in to OIF. Indeed, the biggest hazard we now faced in OSW was not from Iraqi AAA but from the huge number of aircraft now flying in the area. Many of the units that had recently arrived were new to the restricted airspace and the SPINS (special instructions) unique to OSW and the NAG. In the "Box", it was common to fly 1000-ft passes with other Coalition aircraft at night, having spotted them late on NVGs due to the minimal aircraft lighting employed. It was danger-

ous, but manageable with strict adherence to SPINS, which stipulated geographical and altitude deconfliction.

'We also got to drop a lot more bombs in our second phase of OSW than we had first time round. The air wing had conducted a large number of ROs upon initially arriving in-theatre in late October, but these had tailed off by the time we left for the first time in early December. Things then picked up as we began to prep the battlefield in the south in the final weeks before the war.

'My last bomb drop in OSW was a Time Critical Target mission that saw my wingman and I given the word to launch when we were asleep in our bunks! We were manning the alert jets on an OSW no-fly day when patrolling Coalition aircraft informed CAOC that they had detected a violation of the No-Fly Zone. Just two hours after being given the shake to wake up, we were dropping bombs on the target in southern Iraq. The good thing about this mission was that the air wing had been stood down, so we got to launch without any delays, hit the target and then recover, all without having to take on fuel from a tanker. The whole flight lasted

VFA-113's Lt Cdr Sean Williams glances over his shoulder to check the location of his wingman as he leads his section into southern Iraq in early March 2003. Williams' Hornet carries a 2000-lb GBU-31(V)2/B JDAM on its starboard pylon. A second JDAM would be bolted onto the port outer pylon, mirroring the weapon load-out of his wingman's F/A-18C (*Lt Cdr Sean Williams*)

The KC-10s of the USAF's Air Mobility Command were regularly visited by Navy TACAIR jets during both OSW and OIF. Here, an LGB-toting VFA-115 F/A-18E escorts a KC-10A of the 305th AMW's 2nd ARS, flying out of Al Udeid air base, in Qatar, in February 2003 (*VFA-115*)

less than an hour. We were given this mission because the air force was not flying that day either.'

Lincoln's considerable exposure to OSW allowed its air wing to bed down prior to the commencement of OIF. VFA-115 CO Cdr Jeffrey Penfield felt that the experience his squadron gained operating in the NAG, particularly in February and early March, served it well in the subsequent conflict;

'OSW was of real benefit to VFA-115, as it allowed everyone to get used to operating from the boat in the Gulf. The pilots got to learn the airspace really well, getting to grips with talking to the various

controlling agencies, and the procedures that they followed, as the course rules that were applied in OIF were similar to those we observed in OSW.

'We also got the chance to familiarise ourselves with how systems such as the radar warning receiver, jammers, chaff and flare expendables and radios functioned in real world ops, as opposed to how we trained with them in peacetime. We became so familiar with how these things worked that their operation became habit patterns when we actually got into doing something like attacking a target or avoiding SAMs and AAA. Therefore, once the war started we had all the procedural aspects of both the campaign and the aircraft "suitcased", and this allowed the squadron to enjoy a fairly seamless transition from OSW into OIF. The biggest change for us was that the sortie rate increased dramatically.'

The final carrier to arrive in the NAG for OIF was the Navy's oldest frontline fighting vessel, the USS *Kitty Hawk* (CV-63). Permanently forward-deployed in Japan, the ship is home to CVW-5. Amongst the Hornet pilots embarked in the 'Battle Star Catlactica', as CV-63 was dubbed by its commanding officer, Capt Thomas Parker, was VFA-192 'Golden Dragons' pilot Lt John Allison;

'CVW-5 had been on deployment with the *Kitty Hawk* from September through to December 2002, and we were not supposed to head back out to sea until the early spring of 2003. We got the word just before going on Christmas leave that a late March departure date was changing to a late January, two weeks or longer, at-sea period! Early in the new year CVW-5 conducted an intense period of Field Carrier Landing Practice on Iwo Jima, immediately after which we all got carrier qualified aboard the ship. The air wing then dropped some bombs on a range off Okinawa as part of a general air wing work-up in the area, VFA-192 practising the tactics it would use if war was declared with Iraq. We were then deemed ready to go.'

In early February the Secretary of Defense Donald Rumsfeld signed *Kitty Hawk's* deployment order, and by the end of the month the vessel had taken up station in the far north of the NAG, preparing for its role as the dedicated Close Air Support (CAS) carrier.

Despite having a truncated work up, CVW-5, aboard USS *Kitty Hawk* (CV-63), lived up to its permanently deployed status by fitting seamlessly into CAOC's OSW ATO upon the carrier's arrival in the NAG on 26 February 2003. Designated the CAS carrier for OIF, CV-63's trio of Hornet units still managed to carry out a handful of ROs prior to the invasion of Iraq. Launching on a night mission from bow cat three on the eve of war, VFA-192's 'Dragon 301' (Lot XVI F/A-18C BuNo 164905) powers away from the carrier in afterburner. Initially issued to VFA-146 in early 1994, this aircraft was part of the August 1998 Hornet swap between CVW-9 and CVW-5 that saw VFA-192 receive 12 Lot XVI F/A-18Cs from the 'Blue Diamonds', which in turn took charge of the 'World Famous Golden Dragons'' older Lot XII jets. At the same time that this swap was taking place, VFA-195 also completed a similar exchange of aircraft with VFA-146's sister unit, VFA-147, replacing its Lot XII machines with a mix of Lot XVI and XVII airframes (*PH3 Todd Frantom*)

During the latter half of February, with all three carriers operating within the OSW framework, more and more targets in southern Iraq were attacked by Navy jets. These included strikes on fortified positions along the Kuwaiti border and in the Al Faw peninsula, as well as the destruction of Ababil-100 battlefield missile and Astros-2 multi-barrel rocket launchers near Basra. 'Flat Face' and 'Pluto' early warning radar sites at airfields in western Iraq such as H-3 were also targeted as JTF/SWA endeavoured to make sure that its aircraft controlled the skies over the south. VFA-115's Cdr Jeffrey Penfield elaborated on the drive to secure air supremacy in the lead up to war;

'Prior to OIF starting, we were confident that we had air superiority south of the "33 north line". With the invasion plan for the campaign requiring us to have it in order to ensure the successful insertion of troops on the ground, we wanted to make sure that we did indeed control the skies in the south, so things began to get progressively busier the closer we got to "A-Day".

'There were some very specific objectives for OIF, and these relied on Coalition airpower owning the skies to ensure that the troops on the ground could work unimpeded. The bosses had made it clear to us early on that they were not going to accept any "bad guy" aeroplanes getting in amongst our troops, so there were some key command, control and

CVW-5 also flew its fair share of DCA missions in the final three weeks of OSW as CAOC probed the Iraqi air defences south of the '33 north line'. Heading off on a long patrol (note its three drop tanks), VFA-195 Lot XVI F/A-18C BuNo 164900 is armed with a single AIM-7M Sparrow III under each wing, two AIM-9Ms on the LAU-7 wingtip launchers and a fuselage-mounted AIM-120C. 'Chippy 410' was assigned to Lt Nathan White, who was killed by a PAC-3 Patriot missile on 2 April 2003 while flying 'Chippy 405' (BuNo 164974) (*PH3 Todd Frantom*)

Also configured for DCA, VFA-137's 'Falcon 405' (Block XV F/A-18C BuNo 164693) has a more common missile load-out of three AIM-120Cs and two AIM-9Ms. The Navy's very first Block XV Hornet, this jet was delivered to VFA-137 fresh from the factory in October 1992 (*VFA-137*)

communication nodes that we had to take out so as to maintain our air superiority in the south.'

JTF/SWA had good reason to be concerned about the capabilities of the Iraqi Air Force, for in the final weeks prior to the commencement of hostilities it was generating as many as 150 fast jet flights per day in the central zone not policed by Coalition forces.

JDAM – WEAPON OF CHOICE

The Joint Direct Attack Munition was undoubtedly CAOC's weapon of choice for OSW post-OEF thanks to it being wholly autonomous after release, unlike laser-guided or electro-optical munitions whose accuracy can be affected by bad weather or poor targeting solutions. A clinically accurate weapon against fixed targets, which proliferated in OSW, JDAM is effectively a standard Mk 82, 83 or 84 unguided bomb fitted with a global positioning system (GPS) guidance control unit (GCU), mid-body ventral strakes and a tail unit that has steerable control fins.

Developed by precision weapons pioneer Boeing in the mid to late 1990s, the JDAM differs from other GPS-guided weapons (AGM-130 and EGBU-15) in that it guides completely autonomously after being released – it cannot be steered or fed updated targeting data.

The 'baseline' JDAM is considered to be a 'near precision' weapon, the bomb's GCU relying on a three-axis Inertial Navigation System (INS) and a GPS receiver to provide its pre-planned or in-flight targeting capability. The INS is a back-up system should the GPS lose satellite reception or be jammed. With GPS guidance at its heart, the JDAM can only be employed by an aircraft fitted with an on-board GPS system so that GPS-computed coordinates can be downloaded to the weapon for both the target itself and the weapon release point. That way, the jet's onboard INS remains as accurate as possible while the weapon is acquiring a GPS signal after being released over the target.

This effectively means that the jet has to have a MIL-STD 1760 data bus and compatible pylon wiring in order to programme the bomb's aim point, intended trajectory shape and impact geometry.

All this information will have been loaded by the pilot onto his MU (Memory Unit, built into the F/A-18C) or MDL (Mission Data Loader, employed by the F/A-18A+ and F/A-18E/F) via the TAMPS (Tactical Aircrew Mission Planning System) pre-flight, should the jet be going after a fixed target. If, however, a target of opportunity crops up once the aircraft has launched, the pilot simply has to enter its GPS coordinates into the F/A-18's mission computer and the bomb's aim point is automatically altered.

Achieving initial operational capability in 1997, JDAM made its frontline debut during the NATO-led bombing campaign in Serbia and Kosovo during Operation *Allied Force* in 1999. It was then progressively employed during OSW primarily by the US Navy, until the weapon really began to capture headlines during OEF thanks to the exploits of naval Hornet units operating from the various carriers assigned to the conflict. JDAM did not make its combat debut with the F-14B until February 2002, again in OEF, and on the eve of OIF with the F-14D – the A-model Tomcat could not employ JDAM because of the jet's lack of a digital data bus.

VFA-137's 'CAG bird' (Lot XV
F/A-18C BuNo 164712) is stroked
down waist cat four on 12 February
2003. The Hornet is armed with a
JDAM and standard defensive
AAMs. 'Falcon 400' was delivered to
VFA-137 on 10 February 1993, the
aircraft having the distinction of
being the 10,000th TACAIR jet built
by McDonnell Douglas. Next in line
to launch is the unit's CO jet, Lot XV
F/A-18C BuNo 164698 (which is also
featured in Mark Postlethwaite's
specially commissioned cover
artwork). Flying an oversized 'Old
Glory' from its foremast, the
Ticonderoga class cruiser USS
Mobile Bay (CG-53) has closed up to
the carrier in order to flash a signal
to the bridge of CV-64. Assigned to
the *Constellation* battle group,
Mobile Bay was one of five guided
missile cruisers to launch PGM-109
Tomahawk Land Attack Missiles
against 45 fixed targets in Iraq on
the night of 20-21 March 2003 as
part of 'Shock and Awe' (*US Navy*)

As in OSW and then OIF, OEF saw Navy strike units uploading known grid coordinates of static targets into the TAMPS aboard the carrier, and these were in turn transferred to the Hornet's mission computer via the MU or MDL. Once the target sets had been downloaded, the aircraft would allocate single aim points to each J-weapon prior to launch. Employment of the Hornet's radar and NITE Hawk Forward-Looking Infra-Red (FLIR) pod, as well as other external data links and/or secure radio communication from Forward Air Controllers on the ground or in the air, E-2s, E-3s, E-8 JSTARS, RC-135s or RQ-1 Predator UAVs allowed the pilot to re-programme his JDAM in flight.

Aside from its stunning accuracy in OEF, the weapon also proved popular with crews because it could be released in level flight from high altitude, thus allowing jets to stay well above any SAM or AAA threats. Depending on the height and speed of the delivery platform, JDAM can be released up to 15 miles away from its target in ideal conditions.

Following several embarrassing targeting failures of LGBs in OSW in the late summer of 2002, including one weapon which almost severed an oil pipeline, CAOC began to favour the employment of JDAM weaponry almost exclusively. This continued up until the final battlefield prepping in February 2003. One of those impressed by the J-weaponry he employed in-theatre prior to OSW was CVW-2's Capt Mark Fox;

'To illustrate just how revolutionary J-weapons are, and how they have shaped how we deploy our forces, in my first combat mission in *Desert Storm* I dropped four Mk 84 dumb bombs on a hangar at H-3 airfield in western Iraq, and in my first deployment of J-weapons on OSW on 26 December 2002, I placed three JDAM on three widely spaced aim points. These weapons have effectively changed the Navy's mission mindset from how many sorties per target to how many targets per sortie.

'JDAM has also changed the way air wings prepare their bombing missions. In a classic old-fashioned air wing (*text continues on page 33*)

25

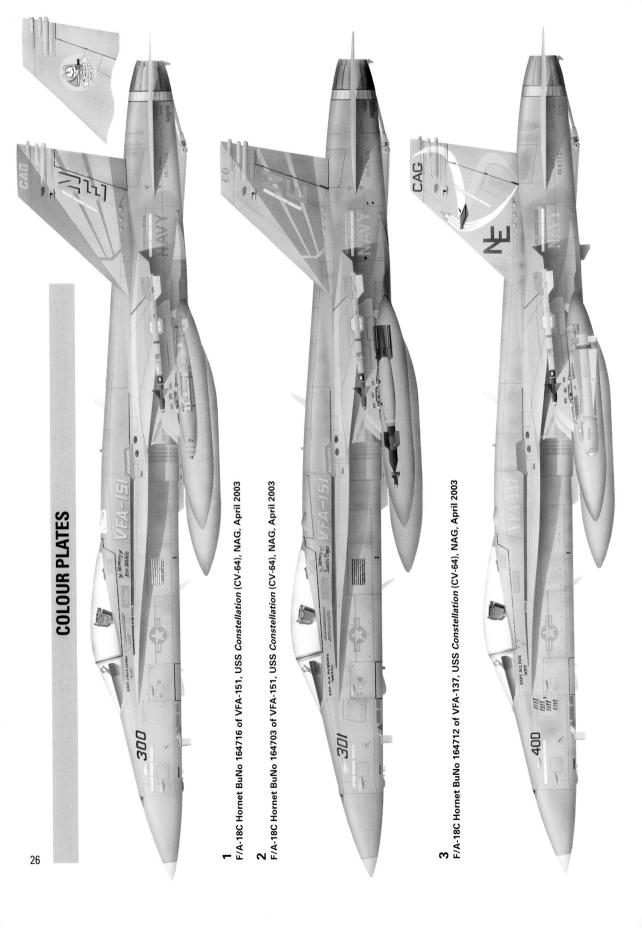

COLOUR PLATES

1
F/A-18C Hornet BuNo 164716 of VFA-151, USS *Constellation* (CV-64), NAG, April 2003

2
F/A-18C Hornet BuNo 164703 of VFA-151, USS *Constellation* (CV-64), NAG, April 2003

3
F/A-18C Hornet BuNo 164712 of VFA-137, USS *Constellation* (CV-64), NAG, April 2003

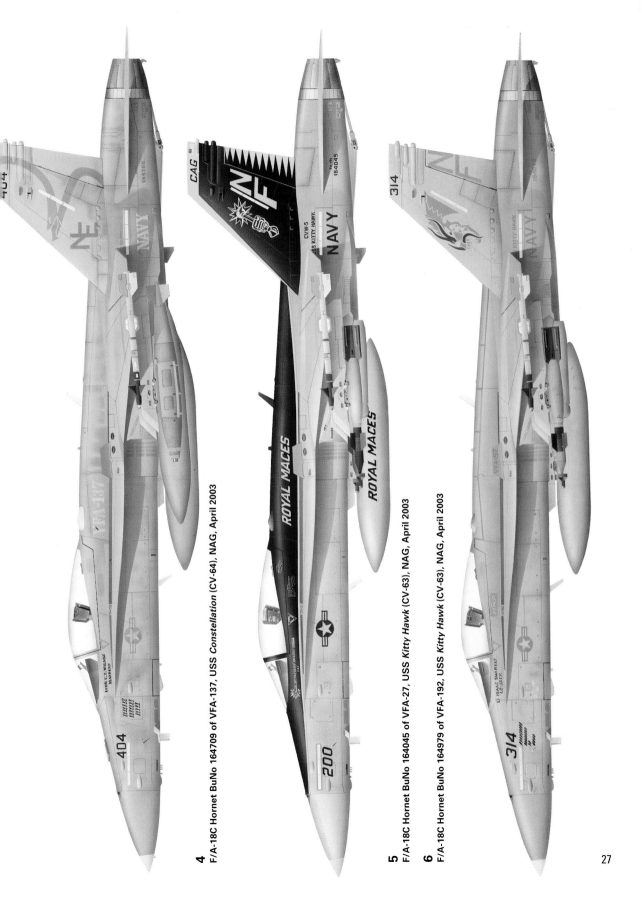

4
F/A-18C Hornet BuNo 164709 of VFA-137, USS *Constellation* (CV-64), NAG, April 2003

5
F/A-18C Hornet BuNo 164045 of VFA-27, USS *Kitty Hawk* (CV-63), NAG, April 2003

6
F/A-18C Hornet BuNo 164979 of VFA-192, USS *Kitty Hawk* (CV-63), NAG, April 2003

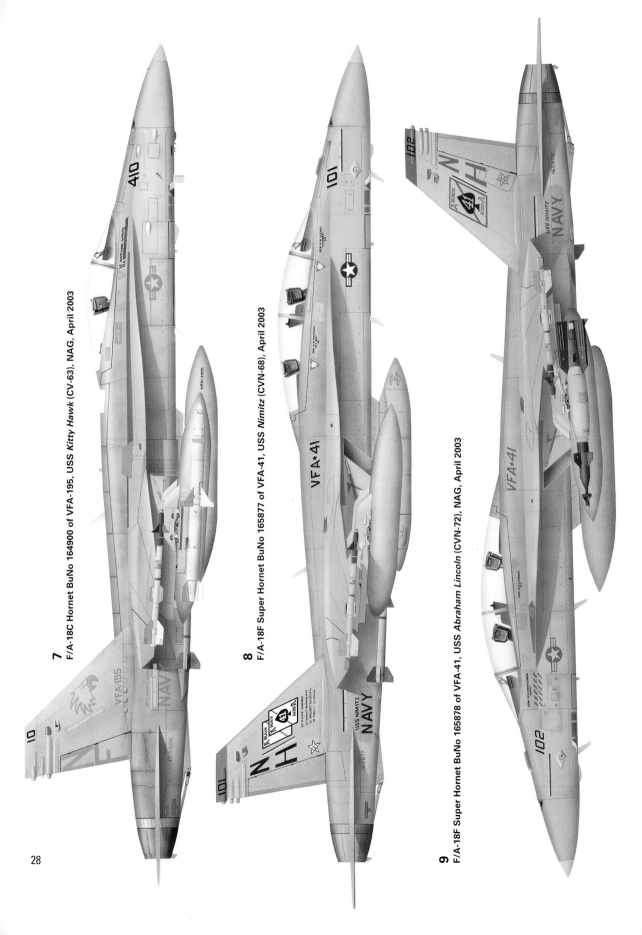

7
F/A-18C Hornet BuNo 164900 of VFA-195, USS *Kitty Hawk* (CV-63), NAG, April 2003

8
F/A-18F Super Hornet BuNo 165877 of VFA-41, USS *Nimitz* (CVN-68), April 2003

9
F/A-18F Super Hornet BuNo 165878 of VFA-41, USS *Abraham Lincoln* (CVN-72), NAG, April 2003

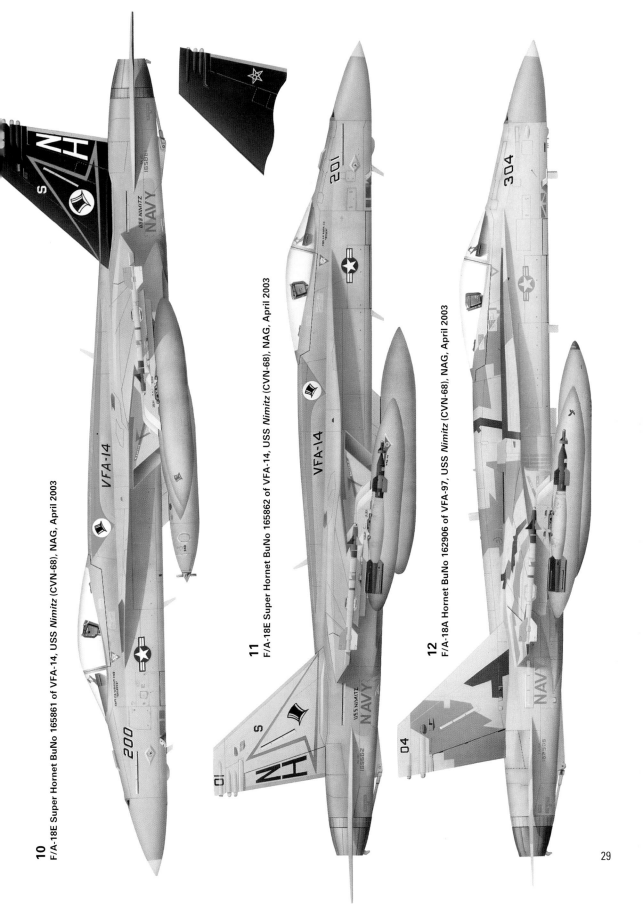

10
F/A-18E Super Hornet BuNo 165861 of VFA-14, USS *Nimitz* (CVN-68), NAG, April 2003

11
F/A-18E Super Hornet BuNo 165862 of VFA-14, USS *Nimitz* (CVN-68), NAG, April 2003

12
F/A-18A Hornet BuNo 162906 of VFA-97, USS *Nimitz* (CVN-68), NAG, April 2003

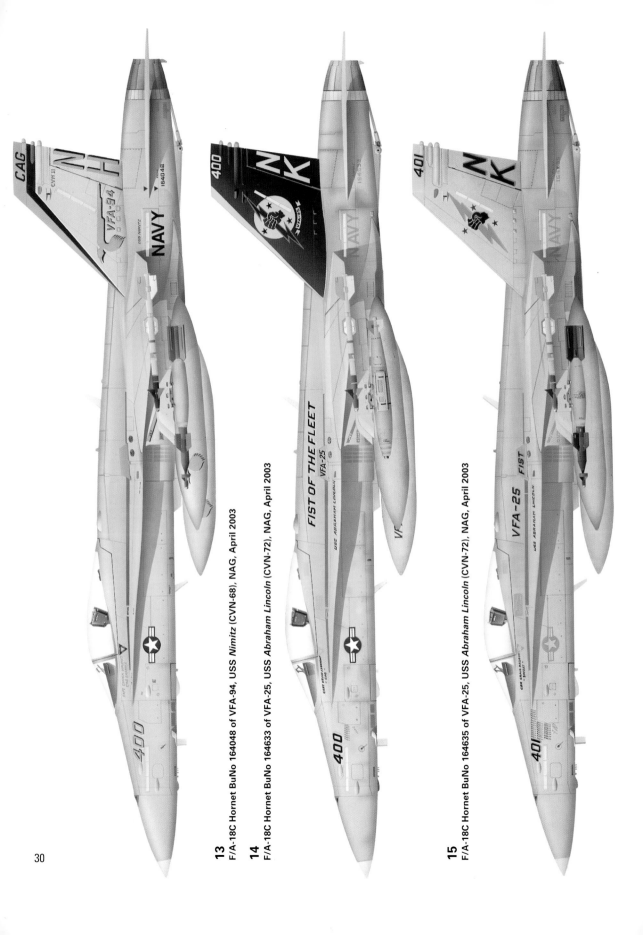

13
F/A-18C Hornet BuNo 164048 of VFA-94, USS *Nimitz* (CVN-68), NAG, April 2003

14
F/A-18C Hornet BuNo 164633 of VFA-25, USS *Abraham Lincoln* (CVN-72), NAG, April 2003

15
F/A-18C Hornet BuNo 164635 of VFA-25, USS *Abraham Lincoln* (CVN-72), NAG, April 2003

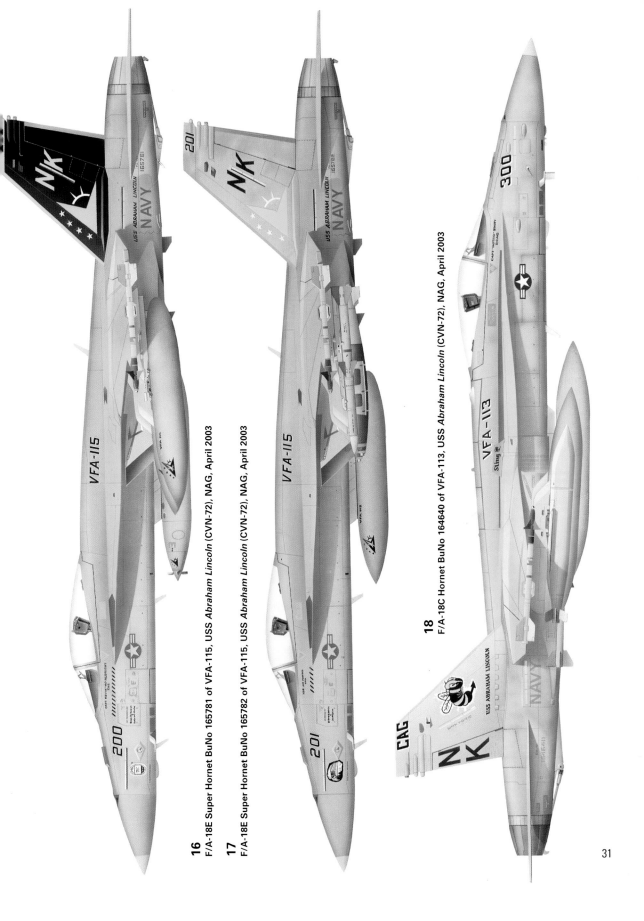

16
F/A-18E Super Hornet BuNo 165781 of VFA-115, USS *Abraham Lincoln* (CVN-72), NAG, April 2003

17
F/A-18E Super Hornet BuNo 165782 of VFA-115, USS *Abraham Lincoln* (CVN-72), NAG, April 2003

18
F/A-18C Hornet BuNo 164640 of VFA-113, USS *Abraham Lincoln* (CVN-72), NAG, April 2003

31

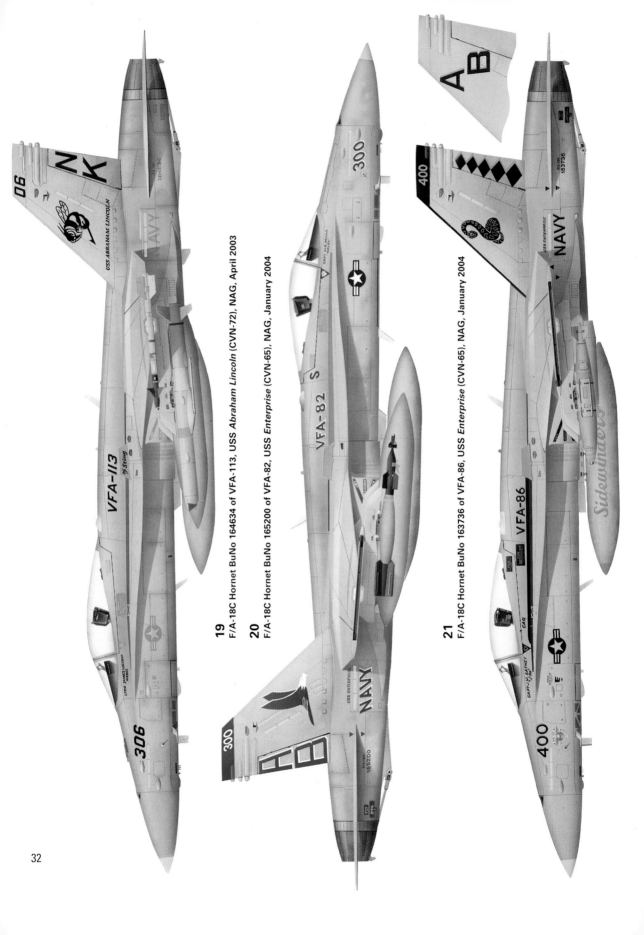

19
F/A-18C Hornet BuNo 164634 of VFA-113, USS *Abraham Lincoln* (CVN-72), NAG, April 2003

20
F/A-18C Hornet BuNo 165200 of VFA-82, USS *Enterprise* (CVN-65), NAG, January 2004

21
F/A-18C Hornet BuNo 163736 of VFA-86, USS *Enterprise* (CVN-65), NAG, January 2004

strike, you would sit there for hours studying every little detail of the target. Now, you will of course still perform some target study, but it is not down to my physical skills as an attack pilot that the ordnance hits the target – accurate GPS coordinates facilitate that part of the mission. You can choose a whole host of targets to hit with JDAM, and your ability to strike them accurately will not be adversely affected by weather conditions. As long as you have precise latitude and longitude coordinates for the GPS, then you can service those targets.'

EVE OF WAR

With diplomatic efforts by the UN failing to secure a peaceful solution to the Iraqi crisis, and Saddam Hussein ignoring an ultimatum by the US government to flee his country, war seemed inevitable by mid March 2003. There were now more than 300,000 Coalition troops in-theatre ready to invade Iraq, their drive north being supported by 1800 aircraft – 700 of which were Navy and Marine Corps machines.

Aside from the three carriers in the NAG, the USS *Theodore Roosevelt* (CVN-71) and USS *Harry S Truman* (CVN-75) were now also on station in the eastern Mediterranean ready to support the war in the north.

One of the pilots who got an early insight into how the conflict in Iraq was going to be fought was Cdr Greg Fenton of CVN-71-based VFA-15;

'My CAG "chose" me to go into the CAOC in "PSAB", which I joined three weeks prior to the kick-off of OIF. I really didn't want this job, but I was chosen because I was the junior XO in CVW-8. I was given the responsibility of writing the 48- to 24-hour flight schedules for all five Navy aircraft carriers. Originally, I was to work on the schedules for the two Mediterranean carriers only, but I wound up creating the OIF air plan for all five carriers. I would work the night shift, and when the ATO came out I would devise the carrier schedules. I had a recalled Navy reservist as my counterpart during the day, but the timing of the publication of the daily ATO effectively meant that the bulk of the air plan was written at night. I remained in this role for the first two weeks of OIF, as senior commanders wanted to keep a planning continuance in place in order to ensure the smooth running of the air war.'

The air wings operating from the NAG continued to attack targets in the southern No-Fly Zone right up until OSW was replaced by OIF.

The LGBs was the weapon of choice for the precision CAS mission, and CVW-5 employed plenty of GBU-12s once the ground phase of OIF got underway. A number of LGBs were also expended during the prepping of the battlefield in the final days of OSW, CVW-5 attacking command, control and communication sites, surface-to-surface missile batteries and an air traffic control radar near Basra. Long-range Type 59 field guns in the Al Faw peninsula and Voest-Alpine GHN-45 155 mm howitzers near Az Zubayr were also knocked out. One of the units involved in these missions on 19 March 2003 was VFA-27, whose 'Mace 205' (Lot XII F/A-18C BuNo 163996) is seen here launching from CV-63's waist cat three with a single 500-lb GBU-12 LGB attached to each outer wing pylon. Reflecting the reduced level of aerial threat in southern Iraq even during OSW, this aircraft is carrying just a single AIM-9M on its starboard wingtip rail and a fuselage-mounted AIM-120C. VFA-27 flew the oldest F/A-18Cs committed to OIF, with this particular jet being the most senior of the 12 sent into combat by the 'Royal Maces'. BuNo 163996 was delivered to the Navy in November 1989, initially being issued to CVW-11's VFA-22. It was passed on to VFA-27 in early 1996 when the unit transitioned from Alpha to Charlie model Hornets at NAS Lemoore. Several months later BuNo 163996 journeyed west to NAF Atsugi, Japan, when VFA-27 joined CVW-5 (*PH3 Todd Frantom*)

Amongst the pilots involved in these final prepping missions was VFA-192's Lt John Allison, whose air wing (CVW-5) had been tasked with operating closely with ground forces;

'We performed daylight RO strikes for the Army and Marines in the hours leading up to the first missions to Baghdad, attacking Republican Guard barracks, HQ buildings, mobile missile launchers and AAA and missile sites in and around Basra. Our Hornets employed mixed loads of JDAM and LGBs, with the ordnance dropped being weather dependent.'

These missions had taken place on 19 March, just hours before the surprise decapitation strike was launched on Baghdad by 40 Tomahawk Land Attack Missiles (TLAMs) and two USAF F-117s from the 8th Expeditionary Fighter Squadron. Amongst the tactical targets hit by CVW-5 during the day and CVW-2 that evening were command, control and communication sites, surface-to-surface missile batteries and an air traffic control radar near Basra, as well as long-range Type 59 field guns in the Al Faw peninsula and Voest-Alpine GHN-45 155 mm howitzers near Az Zubayr.

That same day, CVW-14 and CVW-2 had conducted precision strike missions in support of Special Forces (reportedly pre-positioned in Jordan) in their endeavours to capture H-2 and H-3 airfields in Iraq's western desert, and to neutralise the Scud threat against Israel. VFA-151's Lt Cdr Ron Candiloro was on one of CVW-2's final night missions to western Iraq, his formation having launched from CV-64 in the pre-dawn hours of 20 March – at around the same time as the F-117 decapitation strikers departed their base at Al Udeid, in Qatar;

'Myself and three other pilots in my division of four Hornets claimed to have dropped the very first bombs of OIF, as when President Bush actually made the announcement that we were executing our attacks, the four of us were up in north-western Iraq bombing a Republican Guard barracks. Therefore, although we were not involved in the first strikes on Baghdad, we almost certainly dropped the first bombs of the conflict proper. We had no AAA opposition on this mission, the barracks being sited in a small town in the middle of literally nowhere. The sun was beginning to rise behind us, and as we closed on the target I knew that the soldiers in the barracks had no clue that we were coming. We soon announced our presence, however, with a series of pinpoint strikes.'

Operation *Iraqi Freedom* was well and truly underway by the time Lt Cdr Candiloro's division recovered back aboard the 'Connie'.

VFA-151 also attacked targets in western Iraq during the last OSW missions generated by CENTCOM, striking airfields at H-2 and H-3 and Republican Guard barracks in the pre-dawn hours of 20 March. Heading out on a daylight mission in early March, 'Switch 306' (Lot XV F/A-18C BuNo 164713) is armed with a single GBU-12 LGB on the starboard outer pylon, a GBU-35(V)1/B JDAM on the port outer pylon (unseen), a pair of AIM-9Ms and a solitary AIM-120C. This was a standard war load for Hornets from CVW-2 in the final weeks of OSW. Delivered to the Navy by McDonnell Douglas in March 1993, this aircraft has served exclusively with VFA-151. In that time it has completed five OSW deployments, the last of which evolved, of course, into OIF (*VFA-151*)

'SHOCK AND AWE'

The US government pre-empted the official start of Operation *Iraqi Freedom* by carrying out a daring precision bombing strike on Baghdad on the morning of 20 March 2003. This raid by two F-117s on three homes (or a bunker in a Republican Guard compound, according to certain reports) owned by members of the Iraqi leadership in a suburb on the outskirts of Baghdad, had been hastily generated following a tip off that Saddam Hussein and four of his top commanders had been seen entering these buildings. Although the targets were destroyed by four EGBU-27 'Have Void' 2000-lb LGBs, the intelligence proved to be incorrect and Saddam remained very much alive.

With OSW now a thing of the past, the carrier air wings in the NAG and the eastern Mediterranean prepared to undertake the so-called 'Shock and Awe' phase of the campaign. War planners in the Pentagon had put forward this tactical model – officially referred to as OPLAN 1003V – to the US government as being the best way to ensure that OIF was a swift campaign with minimal collateral damage to civilians.

Rapid domination of the enemy was at the heart of 'Shock and Awe', and senior US commanders explained to President Bush and Secretary of Defence Donald Rumsfeld that this could only be achieved by the world's lone post-Cold War superpower mounting an intense bombardment in the opening days of the war. This would show the Iraqis just how great Coalition firepower was, and prove to them that resistance was useless.

CVW-2's Capt Mark Fox had been given a high-level briefing in early February on how OIF was originally to be fought;

'The plan called for an air campaign kicked off with a massive airstrike ("A-Day", and the beginning of "Shock and Awe"), followed a few days later by the ground war ("G-Day"). The plan evolved, however, as the conflict grew nearer. The gap between "A-" and "G-Days" became progressively smaller, with good reason – days of heavy airstrikes would give the Iraqis the opportunity to sabotage their domestic oilfields and offshore oil platforms before our ground forces could intervene.

'The opening strike – consisting of multiple salvos of cruise missiles and Coalition strike aircraft – targeted hundreds of aim points in several sequential waves, making the first hours of OIF the most overwhelming delivery of precision ordnance ever seen. Designed to saturate and destroy Iraqi air defences, roll back the Baghdad SuperMEZ (Missile Engagement Zone), destroy key command and control nodes and degrade the ground forces' ability to defend Baghdad, the opening strike was pretty impressive for a single evening's work.'

Despite hitting a large number of pre-planned targets on 'A-Day', it appears that the scope of 'Shock and Awe' was deliberately scaled back on the advice of senior military figures in-theatre such as Gen Tommy Franks, Commander of CENTCOM, who was keen to see potential targets such as bridges, water and electricity networks and telephone systems left untouched. This change of tack appears to have come at the eleventh hour, for reports emanating from Washington, D.C. in late January 2003 spoke of a plan to fire some 800 TLAMs at targets in Baghdad in the first 48 hours of the campaign alone, with aircraft striking a further 3000 listed targets during this period. Instead, CENTCOM's statistics from the war indicate that only about 320 TLAMs (out of a total of 802 for the entire war) were launched on 20/21 March, with the bulk of these preceding the 'A-Day' air strikes on Baghdad on the 21st.

Although not expressly told that the campaign strategy had been changed, aircrew on carriers in the NAG quickly realised that their pre-war expectations of how intense the opening phase of OIF would be were wrong. Lt Cdr Ron Candiloro's recollection of the first few days of the war for VF-151 was typical of most of the Hornet pilots that the author interviewed while writing this book;

'Fifth Fleet boss Adm Timothy Keating came out to the ship in early March, and he gave us all a big brief on how the war was going to be fought. The initial plan, as it was explained to us, was that we were going to execute a huge number of sorties that would see us simply fly, eat and sleep. However, when OIF did finally start, CENTCOM throttled back on the number of strike sorties we were tasked to fly, so the war itself was not nearly as intense as we thought it was going to be in terms of the number of missions that we flew. Each pilot was looking at flying two or three times a day, based on the pre-war briefing, but we ended up flying once a day instead. This proved to be a comfortable pace for us, as it allowed us to do other things aside from flying, eating and sleeping.'

In a portent of things to come, the only significant Hornet operations in the immediate aftermath of the decapitation strike involved units from CVW-5 and CVW-14, who conducted a series of Close-Air Support (CAS) missions for elements of the 1st Marine Division and the British Army's 1st Armoured Division in their push on Basra. To the north, Hornets also helped clear the way for the US Army's V Corps (3rd Division) as its mechanised units raced across the desert towards a strategic bridge that spanned the Euphrates River at An Nasiriyah.

Although primarily supported by land-based Marine TACAIR and AV-8Bs operating from 'Harrier carriers' in the NAG, the 1st Marine Expeditionary Force (MEF) also called on naval TACAIR during the capture of the Rumaylah oilfield in the Al Faw Peninsula. Elsewhere in

CVW-5 launched a series of CAS strikes in support of elements of the 1st Marine Division and the British Army's 1st Armoured Division in their push on Basra in the pre-dawn hours of 20 March 2003. To the north, Hornets from CV-63 also helped clear the way for the US Army's V Corps (3rd Division) as its mechanised units headed for a strategic bridge that spanned the Euphrates River at An Nasiriyah. Seconds away from launching off waist cat three on the eve of 'Shock and Awe', VFA-27's 'Mace 206' (Lot XII F/A-18C BuNo 164059) has a single GBU-12 attached to each outer wing pylon (*PH3 Todd Frantom*)

this immediate region, Hornets helped US Navy SEALs and other Special Forces seize the vital port facility at Umm Qasr after a fierce firefight.

Aside from flying these CAS missions in southern Iraq and a series of DCA patrols further north, Navy TACAIR assets in the NAG effectively remained unused for the opening 36 hours of the campaign until the first 'iron jet' strikes were conducted on Baghdad on the evening of 21 March.

Preparation for the 'A-Day' attacks on fixed targets in the Iraqi capital had dominated air wing planning in the lead up to OIF, as Capt Mark Fox recalled;

'In early March, the CAOC assigned Mission Commander responsibilities for the opening strike to CVW-2 based on our schedule. Since the campaign began at night ("H-hour" called for the first bombs to fall on their target at 2100 hrs local), and would be sustained around the clock, we as the night carrier were well situated to conduct flight operations for the first 18 hours of the conflict. And since I was CAG, it was my job to lead the strike. Having spent my entire career in tactical aviation preparing for just this moment, I was in exactly the right place at precisely the right time, and was humbled by the honour.

'Not knowing exactly when "A-Day" was kept our head in the game. We coordinated the opening strike with both the CAOC and every Coalition entity involved – CVW-5 and -14 in the NAG, USAF F-15Cs, F-15Es, F-16CJs, B-2s, F-117s, land-based "concrete" EA-6Bs and RAF Tornado GR 4s. Improved communications – voice, data and video-tele-conference – were priceless, as coordination that would have taken weeks using military messages happened in hours and minutes. Among other things, we maintained 24-hour connectivity with the CAOC in the Current Operations cell, which gave us the ability to understand what they were thinking when there were glitches in the ATO.

'The major problem facing us that first night was how to create a plan that provided suitable deconfliction between strike aircraft, and which still allowed us to service all the targets that needed to be hit. The first OIF strike was not the place to have a mid-air collision, and with 50 bomb-dropping jets assigned to this mission, the chances of this occurring were high if the deconfliction plan was not a sound one.

'I was able to brief all of the widely spread assets participating in this first mission thanks to SIPRNET, the secret internet system that has dramatically improved our ability to connect and communicate. SIPRNET allowed me to shoot my game plan for deconfliction out to all the different mission commanders in the various participating units. This in turn gave them the opportunity to come back with a request to go higher or lower, and I could quickly build up my vertical deconfliction plan.

'Ready Room Five on CV-64 was crowded – standing room only – for the late afternoon strike brief on

CVW-2's mission planners conduct a mini-brief for the opening strike of 'Shock and Awe' in VF-2's ready room on 21 March 2003. The graphics on the projection screens show the Baghdad SuperMEZ, as well as other SAM threat areas around the cities north of the Iraqi capital. The zonal range for each missile system has been individually colour coded on both slides (*US Navy*)

Photographed through a night vision filter, 'ordies' from VFA-151 carefully manoeuvre a 2000-lb GBU-31(V)2/B JDAM into position beneath the port outer wing pylon of 'Switch 314' (Lot XV F/A-18C BuNo 164879) aboard CV-64 during the evening of 21 March 2003. This aircraft was one of two VFA-151 jets that participated in the follow up CVW-2 'Shock and Awe' strike on a barracks complex in Karbala, which was led by 'Vigilantes' CO, Cdr Mark Hubbard (*US Navy*)

'Big wing' tankers played a key role in the 'Shock and Awe' phase of OIF, boosting the range of the notoriously 'short-legged' legacy Hornet to such an extent that units operating from vessels in the NAG could reach targets in and around Baghdad. Tankers were always in short supply, however. This VFA-151 jet is topping off its tanks prior to heading into Iraq (*VFA-151*)

21 March 2003. There was a hushed atmosphere and an unmistakable feeling of "this is it" as the 25 embedded journalists aboard the "Connie" squeezed into the ready room alongside the aviators for the brief.

'I briefed the strike earlier than normal in order to establish an unhurried atmosphere of clinical, calculated, deliberate professionalism. There was no need to make any "win one for the Gipper" motivational speeches – everyone's head was in the game tonight.

'We had four waves scheduled to attack Baghdad. I had the TLAMs (fired from naval vessels in the NAG) go in first, followed by the Hornets carrying JSOW, then the low signature stealth jets and finally the "iron" aeroplanes – F/A-18Cs and F-14Ds – loaded with JDAM. The latter wave would be immediately preceded by heavy radar jamming from the numerous EA-6Bs in the area.

'For me and my element, the launch was smooth, the flow to the tankers exactly as planned and the weather – for the first wave at least – benign. Having worked carefully on this plan, I knew each element by call-sign as they checked in. Using NVGs, I watched the multiple dozens of aircraft, launched from three carriers and several land bases, proceed to their tanker tracks and into Iraq as if we had practised it a dozen times. It was like flying over the US eastern seaboard or Los Angeles on a busy night – and tonight was a very busy night indeed – but with no air traffic control centre to coordinate and deconflict our flightpaths.

'We had devised a simple plan in order to deal with this congestion pre-war, and it essentially took the form of a series of three-dimensional "highways in the skies", complete with off-ramps, reporting points and altitude splits that mitigated the mid-air hazard. Devised with the help of CAOC and CVW-14, my plan called for formations to stay to the right of a waypoint at a certain altitude as per the American rules of the road. Even with this plan in place, the prudent aviator always remained at his designated altitude, did belly checks and kept his head on a swivel when joining the tanker!

'After all the effort to build simple airspace rules in the previous weeks and months, watching the first strike smoothly unfold before me was a beautiful sight to behold.

'Our tanking tracks were over Saudi Arabia, and they were some way south – certainly further south than I would have preferred. Tanking complete and my element formed up, I worked the time-distance problem to Baghdad, with a northwesterly 120-knot jetstream adding variables to my calculations. Near An Najaf, 100 nautical miles south of Baghdad, the high overcast layer receded to reveal a dark, clear night.

'Baghdad – a city the size of Detroit – was faintly visible on the horizon to the naked eye, but brightly lit in green hues when viewed through NVGs. Familiar geography emerged – looking east, the Tigris and Euphrates rivers were defined by the cultural lighting of Iraq's southern towns and cities, while the ink-black expanse of the desert to the west was marked only by an occasional light.

'Things were heating up in the north - our Prowlers started jamming, kicking off the most impressive fireworks display I've ever seen. Dozens of SAMs launched and began to arc gracefully upward, some exploding well above our altitude, others snuffing out in mid-flight. Baghdad's hundreds of AAA sites punctuated the night sky, their random streams of fire and muzzle flashes sparkling like the widespread flash photography in a stadium at the end of the Super Bowl.

'Long range stand-off weapons – a SLAM-ER (Stand-off Land Attack Missile-Expanded Response), launched and guided by two Hornet junior officers from CVW-2, and Tomahawk cruise missiles – arrived precisely as scheduled, and the graphic light show intensified. The TLAMs were truly spectacular, and I had not previously seen these used in combat. Missiles exploded on targets all over the city, hitting literally a hundred aim points in the first wave. All over Baghdad fireworks streaked skyward, and explosions blossomed on the ground. It was a sight to remember.

'Not everything was going as planned, however. While working to get to my JSOW release point on time, I was simultaneously figuring out a way to get all the strikers to their targets in spite of emerging lapses in the Super-MEZ (surface-to-air missile engagement zone) suppression effort. A flight of Hornets carrying anti-radiation missiles had been delayed during tanking and was out of position to fire pre-emptive HARMs in support of a JDAM-carrying Tomcat division.

'The Tomcats – on timeline – would be in the heart of the SuperMEZ without a key element of suppression, but to delay until the HARM shooters arrived would run the F-14s low on gas, add to their overall exposure in the Baghdad area and otherwise disrupt the strike flow. Of all the nights to rely on the Iraqi defences being confused and saturated, this was the one. I told the Tomcats to press on to their targets as planned.

'Baghdad's lights, and the building crescendo of explosions, were almost too bright to view through NVGs. The Iraqi defences were spectacular, but ineffective – none of the SAMs were guiding, no one had any indication of being illuminated by fire control or target tracker radars, and the vast majority of the fireworks were going off below us. An

Safely back aboard CV-64 after leading the first 'iron jet' strike on Baghdad, CVW-2's Capt Mark Fox was quite literally thrust into the media spotlight in the hangar deck upon his return. Having not even had the chance to get out of his survival vest and g-suit, Capt Fox patiently answered media questions. By the start of the war, he was very familiar with the needs of the media embedded aboard the ship, as he explained to the author;

'A group of approximately 25 journalists joined us aboard *Constellation* in early March. Although dealing with their insatiable desire for information added complexity to an already demanding time, I thought the idea of embedding reporters and expanding their access was a stroke of genius. Under *Constellation* Carrier Strike Group Commander Adm Barry Costello's leadership, we began daily press conferences to educate and inform the embarked media members on the myriad of technical issues and warfighting concepts relevant to our mission.

'After debriefing Adm Costello and the intelligence team in CVIC (Carrier Intelligence Center), I did exactly what I had told the air wing's aviators to do after the strike – talk to the embedded journalists. Still in flight gear, with "helmet hair" and oxygen mask imprint still evident, I gave CNN's Frank Buckley a live interview. Quite a contrast to 12 years earlier after my first hop in *Desert Storm*!' (*US Navy*)

occasional nearby AAA burst or SAM explosion above us kept our eyes out of the cockpit and our jets in continuous manoeuvre, however.

'Despite being fully aware of the sheer quantity of SAMs in the Baghdad SuperMEZ, we did not fear them, as we knew that the Iraqis had to keep moving their sites so as to avoid being hit by JSOW and JDAM – we had a clear indication of where virtually all their permanent sites were.

'The Iraqis had perfected their "shoot and scoot" techniques over the many years of OSW, and this persisted in OIF. They knew that they had to keep moving so as to ensure their survival against GPS-targeted weapons. This worked for us, as in order to use the SAM effectively by providing it with radar guidance to the target, the missile operators had to keep calibrating the weapon after launch, which in turn made them vulnerable to GPS bombs and HARM. They were not prepared to take this risk, hence the sheer number of ballistic launches in OIF.

'Having never launched multiple JSOW before, I was relieved when the third consecutive "thunk" indicated a normal release of my last weapon. Wrapping up into a hard "tac-turn" to the right, I glanced straight down from a steep angle of bank and was amazed to see the sparkles of muzzle flashes arrayed below in grid squares. Puzzled at first, then fascinated by the spectacle, I was looking at barrage fire from a unique perspective – directly above hundreds of Iraqi troops deployed along the roads of Baghdad's southern suburbs, firing their weapons straight up into the air. Safe in a sanctuary well above the firestorm below, I thought to myself, "This would be a bad night to go low".

'Heading southeast on a tangent away from Baghdad, I looked back over my left shoulder and stared at the spectacle. The city was almost too bright to view through NVGs, our attack vividly marked by a series of explosions that blossomed sporadically from Baghdad's centre section outward in all directions.'

Flying in Capt Fox's division that night was VFA-151's Lt Cdr Richard Thompson, an experienced Hornet pilot who had rejoined the Navy in late 2001 after being one of hundreds of airline pilots made redundant in the wake of the 11 September 2001 attacks;

'I was the number two jet in a flight of four F/A-18Cs lead by Capt Fox. Our mission was to launch 12 JSOW into the Baghdad area against known Al Samoud surface-to-surface missile sites, thereby protecting the upcoming ground invasion of the Iraqi capital. We launched just after sunset and rendezvoused overhead the ship at 18,000 ft. After we had all joined up and completed our weapons checks, we proceeded to the USAF KC-10 tankers that were stationed over northern Saudi Arabia. It took about an hour to get from the ship to the tanker tracks.

'The transit to the tankers was truly memorable. Most aircraft had their formation lights off, but with NVGs on, the moonlight reflected brightly off the numerous contrails.

Raytheon's AGM-154A Joint Stand-Off Weapon (JSOW) took a back seat to JDAM and the LGB for most of OIF, although its superior defence suppression capabilities made it a 'must have' weapon in the early stages of 'Shock and Awe'. Employed exclusively by the F/A-18, the inertially-guided, GPS-aided gliding submunition dispenser can be launched up to 35 kilometres away from the target. This particular weapon is being wheeled along the deck of CVN-72 on its ubiquitous Aero-12C skid, heading for a CVW-14 F/A-18. Some 65 JSOW were expended by the trio of Hornet units operating from the *Lincoln*, three by VFA-115, 38 by VFA-113 and 24 by VFA-25 (*US Navy*)

It reminded me of the busy nights that I flew airliners into Chicago-O'Hare airport. There were literally hundreds of aircraft and contrails all going to the same place – Baghdad.

'We met up with the KC-10 at the planned time and altitude and topped off for the strike. We had a planned (TOT) (time on target), and it was critical that we hit it exactly. We were heading for the Baghdad SuperMEZ – an area that no Coalition strike aircraft had dared to fly into since *Desert Storm*.

'As we headed towards Baghdad, we could see the AAA and missiles being fired at us, and it appeared that none of the latter were being directed with any type of guidance radar – our radar warning receivers told us that we were being illuminated by search radars only. Barrage fire was seemingly the order of the day for the Iraqis, who made a desperate attempt to literally fill the sky with SAMs and AAA in the hope that a Coalition aircraft would fly into a ribbon of cannon shells or a missile. If they had tried to illuminate us with target-tracking radar, we had plenty of HARM missiles available to protect us during our attack. We were nervous heading into Iraq, but we were confident that our plan, tactics and weapons systems would allow us to get in and get out unscathed, regardless of the enemy's defensive effort.

'And that's just what happened. We reached our launch point, and of the 12 JSOW we attempted to employ, 11 were launched successfully ("Dash-3" had a weapon that failed to launch). Due to the stand-off range of the JSOW, we were not able to get weapon system video for our impacts, and subsequent BHA, but later analysis showed that all the Al Samoud missiles we had targeted were destroyed.'

The JSOW launched by Capt Fox's division were expended in support of two Hornets from VFA-137 and two Tomcats from VF-2 that had dropped bombs on the first Baghdad mission. The strikers were tasked with attacking the Salman Pak AM transmitter radio relay facility at Al Hurriyah, southwest of the Iraqi capital. Leading the mixed division of F/A-18Cs and F-14Ds was VF-2's XO, Cdr Doug Denneny, who noted in his diary;

'Back from an incredible mission. I was the division lead that went into the MEZs. Two F-14Ds, two F/A-18Cs, F-16CJs, F/A-18C HARM support and a bunch of jets outside the MEZs lobbing JSOW. Continuous Iraqi AAA following an impressive, non-stop TLAM and CALCM (Conventional Air-Launched Cruise Missile) show. After the Tomahawks stopped, we went in and were greeted by multiple (10-12) SAMs – all unguided – and non-stop AAA. The latter was mainly low stuff, but some up high too. Had to make a lot of go/no go decisions. Overall, went well. Two of our wingmen couldn't drop, but we got our JDAM off and the same with our "Dash-3", Cdr Walt Stammer, CO of VFA-137. A good

Red anti-collision beacons flashing and night formation 'slime' strips aglow, this VFA-137 jet has been placed under tension on bow cat one and is just seconds away from being launched on CVW-2's first air strike of OIF on 21 March 2003. Armed with three 1000-lb JDAM, this aircraft was one of four VFA-137 Hornets to participate in the mission – two were carrying bombs and two HARMs (*US Navy*)

night, and we are all back safely. Incredible media coverage both before and after the flight. Happy with our unit's overall performance on day one. We are working hard!'

As Cdr Denneny mentions in his diary account of this first OIF mission, one of his division members was Cdr Walt Stammer, who also had vivid memories of this sortie;

'VFA-137 sortied four Hornets as part of the first Baghdad strike, with CVW-2 launching 20 jets in total that ventured north to the Iraqi capital. Some 60 Coalition aircraft attacked in the first wave, and aside from the jets off the "Connie", there were B-1s, B-2s, F-117s, F-15s and F-16s in the sky with us. My four-aircraft division consisted of two jets armed with three 1000-lb JDAM and two with HARMs. Only the two JDAM bombers went into Baghdad with two similarly equipped Tomcats, the remaining VFA-137 jets joining the 14 other F/A-18Cs, F-14Ds and EA-6Bs providing us with EW or DCA support from outside the SuperMEZ.

'Some of our jets also protected F-117s and B-2s on this mission. Operating with the Air Force posed no problems for us, as all the information we required was on the ATO issued to the ship by CAOC in advance of the mission, and as we all stuck rigidly to our target times, the strike went off seamlessly. We deconflicted by altitude and time, and this made sure that we did not get in each others' way. We successfully dropped our ordnance within minutes of the EW jets expending their HARM and JSOW on known missile sites near to our target.

'By far the biggest challenge facing us on that first mission was getting sufficient gas to get to Baghdad and back. The Coalition really struggled to find bases in the area that were capable of operating tankers, and the strike packages began to shrink in size due to a paucity of tankers.'

The same problem affected the second strike to venture north on 'A-Day', which included jets from both CVW-2 and -14. Leading the aircraft from the latter air wing was VFA-25's XO, Cdr Don Braswell, who recalled;

'CVW-14 had been divided up into strike teams, and it so happened that my team was chosen to participate in the wing's first strike on Baghdad. I also included CAG in the strike package, as he was, of course, the senior pilot on the ship. Two regular squadron pilots from VFA-25 were also involved in the strike, and the fourth jet was flown by CTF-50 staffer and CVW-2 D-CAG select, Capt Larry Burt.

'Prior to launching, we had told CAOC that there was not going to be enough fuel on station for everyone to press on into Iraq, and that was exactly what happened. My wingman and I were told as soon as we arrived on station to join up with a tanker that there wasn't enough fuel to go around, so he and I simply got sufficient "gas" to get back to the ship and then headed home. This

CVW-14's first OIF strike was led by VFA-25 XO Cdr Don Braswell, seen here going through his kneeboard 'smart pack' with CTF-50 staffer and CVW-2 D-CAG select Capt Larry Burt during their mission brief. The latter accompanied him on the Baghdad strike, and actually got to drop his bombs on the target. Braswell, however, was forced to return to CVN-72 with his wingman when their 'big wing' tanker ran out of fuel. Information was the key to mission effectiveness and survival in OIF for all TACAIR crews, and in the single-seat F/A-18 it was easy for pilots to quickly become overwhelmed. They had to run the radios, find the tanker, avoid the engagement zones of the Patriot missile batteries and navigate through some truly dreadful weather. Having managed this, they then got to dodge Iraqi AAA and SAMs whilst searching out, and then bombing, their targets. In an effort to reduce the naval aviator's workload, CTF-50 produced a 'smart pack' which proved very useful, as Capt Larry Burt recalled;

'Notebook-sized, it contained every single frequency used in the campaign, as well as the procedures for all the main aspects of a typical combat mission in OIF. Us single-seat guys had that pack highlighted, tabbed and laminated throughout in order to allow us to quickly reference it when on tasking. It proved invaluable' (*US Navy*)

was probably just as well, as my jet suffered a hydraulic pump failure on the return flight to the carrier and I had to shut down an engine – I would not have wanted to do this deep inside Iraq. I ended up flying my first OIF sortie the following day instead.'

VFA-151's Cdr Mark Hubbard also participated in the second strike, his division attacking targets to the south and west of Baghdad;

'My great concern on the first night of OIF was that the element of surprise that we may have enjoyed was going to be spoiled by the fact that my CAG's strike package would be heading down range on its way home 45 minutes prior to my division reaching the target. The "sleeping bear", if ever there was one, would be well and truly awake by the time we arrived.

'I had gone to the warfighters' conference ashore in February, where I had been given the plan for the first strikes of OIF. I then went back to the air wing and briefed the strike leads over and over again in the days leading up to the war. However, the plan changed in the wake of the decapitation sortie, which was flown the day prior to the commencement of "Shock and Awe", and once we started flying our bombing missions, as the forces on the ground moved north far quicker than anyone had expected. This resulted in fixed targets falling off the ATO as quickly as you could add them on! We soon found that we needed more tanker assets, and the advent of poor weather also had an adverse effect on the mission scheduling.

'I was so anxious about my first mission on 21 March that I got no sleep prior to launching. I had flown the day before, then went through the flight planning for the strike I was tasked with leading upon my return to the ship. I eventually went to bed some three hours before I was due to get up and brief the mission, but I ended up just laying there, running through the brief over and over again in my head. The alarm went off and I simply got up and briefed the strike, which was to be flown by four Hornets – we were originally to launch with six, but we lost some targets.

JDAM and HARM sit side-by-side in the CVN-72 hangar bay on 21 March 2003. These weapons were soon taken up to the flight deck and loaded onto waiting Hornets, Tomcats and Prowlers, which expended them during CVW-14's first OIF strike. Three versions of JDAM are visible in this photo, the large three-striped grey bombs in the foreground being the 2000-lb GBU-31(V)4 hardened penetrator variant which proved so effective against bunkers, hardened aircraft shelters and runways. The green bombs with grey 'girdles' are standard 2000-lb GBU-31(V)2/Bs, while the smaller JDAM are 1000-lb GBU-35(V)1/Bs. To the right of the photograph, in the second row, are at least six ADM-141C Improved Tactical Air-Launched Decoys, which would have been launched from TACAIR assets (including the F/A-18) as the strike package approached the Baghdad SuperMEZ. Little has appeared in print on the Navy's employment of ITALD in OIF, although Capt Fox of CVW-2 confirmed that his air wing did not use decoys on the first 'Shock and Awe' strike;

'With stand-off weaponry such as JSOW, HARM, SLAM-ER and, in a limited sense, JDAM available, I was more inclined to use real weapons to help saturate the enemy's Integrated Air Defences instead of decoys' (*US Navy*)

43

Armed with no fewer than three AGM-88 HARM rounds, a F/A-18C from VFA-151 prepares for its cat shot on the night of 21 March 2003. The unit's Lt Cdr Ron Candiloro was one of those to shoot a HARM in the early stages of OIF. He told the author;

'When using the AGM-88, you could be working in conjunction with a Prowler, whose crew had given you the coordinates of a newly detected site in flight prior to you firing the missile. Alternately, and more typically, you would be given the coordinates of a SAM site that had already been located by our intelligence people. This was what happened to me, as I was assigned to a CVW-2 strike package going into Iraq at night following a request from the mission commander to "PSAB" that he had no HARM capability. CAOC in turn contacted my wingman and I, as we were already in the area flying HARM-equipped jets, and we were given the mission tasking as formation "add-ons". The coordinates for the radar sites were passed onto us, and we duly neutralised them as requested.

'This was the first time I had fired a HARM, and my wingman launched his ten seconds after I had activated my weapon. It was a long-range shot, and the missile basically "went up to the moon" after I pressed the trigger. It smoked for a while and then disappeared. We did not see the rounds hit the target because we were so far away. The strikers that we were supporting saw them detonate, however, and they reported explosions' (*US Navy*)

'Sitting in on my brief were around half-a-dozen TV camera crews from the embedded media party on the ship, and their presence made my job a little more difficult as I had to fight to keep my focus on what I was telling my pilots, and avoid straying into classified areas. I performed a 45-minute generic brief for the benefit of the media, where I discussed the specific threats, what we were going to do over the target, weather issues, alternative targets, fall-out plans and abort criteria. This had to be done in such a way that my pilots got some benefit from it, as well as catering for the media. Once this was over, we asked the media to leave and I then spoke about specifics – threat envelopes, weapons being used, evasive techniques, target attack profiles, frequencies and mission waypoints.

'We launched (two VFA-151 and two VMFA-323 jets), took gas from the S-3s and headed north, where we ran into a 130-knot head wind. This really hurt our gas consumption. To make matters worse, my four F-16CJs were late getting off the tanker and I could not raise my Prowler, which was joining us from "PSAB". The SEAD support showed up literally two minutes before we would have been timed out and forced to return home.

'My division then split into two flights of two strikers as we approached Baghdad, the Marine jets heading off to attack a communications target in the west. We later joined up with them south of Baghdad after we had dropped our 2000-lb JDAM on a barracks complex in Karbala, where Iraqi security guards charged with protecting Saddam and his government ministers worked, lived and trained. As we approached the target, we could see the Iraqi capital to the north of us being struck by some of the 300+ TLAMs fired that night, as well as ribbons of AAA criss-crossing the sky. It looked just as bad as I had imagined it would.

'As we all joined up and headed back south, I checked that everyone had dropped everything and that no one had suffered any battle damage. We were all in good shape except for gas, although we had made the decision going in that we would be low coming back out. We knew that there were diversionary fields at Al Jaber and Ali Al Salem, in Kuwait, if things really got bad and we had to divert. I also had a great deal of faith in our organic S-3 tanker support from VS-38, as the "Griffins" had been spot on in arriving on station on time during our OSW missions. Sure enough, they came up on the radio just as we knew they would. However,

we were having a hard time actually seeing them, as the weather had gotten a lot worse, and there were aircraft everywhere.

'My division had gone up north at around 29,000 ft and we had returned at close to 40,000 ft, so we started to idle down to our refuelling height. I could tell that the Marine pilots with me were getting a little nervous due our ever-dwindling fuel state, and by this point we had about two minutes in which to find the S-3s. Just as I found them on my radar, the Marines got on the radio and told me that they were well below bingo fuel and were heading for the divert field. However, I knew from past experience that the fuel indicator in the Hornet will run below zero before the engines flame out – I have been forced to do this on several occasions, and a CAG buddy of mine actually landed with just 100 lbs of "gas" left in his jet.

'We knew that there was a divert field below us, and we had briefed to land ashore if we had less than 1500 lbs of gas aboard. We were below this now, and I talked the Marine pilots in staying around a little longer. I then briefly spotted the S-3s right on our nose, but even with the Vikings' formation lights on, we could not get a lasting visual fix on them even with NVGs, as the visibility was poor due to the worsening weather as we flew south. Finally, at less than a mile, we got a visual fix on the tankers. I let my wingman tank first, as he was a junior guy and I wanted to make sure that he got the gas he needed before I topped off. This ran my reserves down a little lower than I would have liked, but we were soon "gassed up" and on our way back to the ship.

'About a third of my missions in OIF were flown exclusively with the support of organic tankers. I preferred to work with the S-3 guys, as they were familiar with our requirements, and I could rely on them being exactly where we had briefed to meet up. Early in the war, the USAF tankers were in southern Saudi Arabia, and it would take you an hour to reach them, an hour to get to your target and back to the tanker and then an hour to get home. We would drag the S-3s up to the Al Faw peninsula, where they would leave us and return to the ship – they never went over the beach into Iraq during the "Shock and Awe" phase of the war.'

As Cdr Hubbard mentioned in his account, these early strikes were meticulously planned and briefed in much the same way as traditional carrier 'Alpha Strikes' had been in Korea, Vietnam and *Desert Storm*.

VS-38's eight S-3Bs had a very busy war providing organic tanker support for CVW-2's fleet of TACAIR aircraft, and its trio of Hornet squadrons in particular. During the course of OIF, 'Red Griffin' Vikings delivered more than 1.7 million pounds of fuel to the air wing, and squadron CO Cdr Steven Kelly told embedded reporters aboard CV-64, 'I don't think you could do night carrier operations without the S-3. On this deployment to date, we have made a half-dozen to a dozen saves, preventing fighter aircraft from going into the water from lack of fuel' (*VFA-151*)

Laden down with two 500-lb GBU-12 LGBs beneath its port wing, a solitary 1000-lb GBU-35(V)1/B JDAM on the outer starboard pylon, two full 330-US gal drop tanks and three defensive missiles, it is little wonder that the pilot of 'Sting 313' has selected full 'burner for his cat shot. Photographed on 21 March 2003, this VFA-113 Hornet (Lot XIII F/A-18C BuNo 164257) was heading for the large Iraqi airfield complexes in western Iraq (*US Navy*)

A VFA-192 F/A-18C taxies towards the bow of CV-63 upon its return from a successful (note the empty wing pylons) CAS mission in the first few days of OIF. Once chained down, the Hornet will be set upon by the deckcrew, who will refuel and rearm it, replenish the chaff and flare expendables and fix any minor gripes reported by the pilot. If all goes according to plan, and no major technical snags are encountered, the jet will be declared 'up' for its next mission within an hour of arriving back aboard the ship (*PH3 Todd Frantom*)

CVW-2 Operations Officer Lt Cdr Zeno Rausa explained to the author how the various aspects of these complex missions were pulled together at air wing level;

'We devised a strategy whereby most of our strike planning was conducted by our Intel department, thus giving our aircrew time to focus on target study, Blue Force (Coalition) positioning and the enemy threat. Our Intel folks passed the ATO, created kneeboard cards, built target imagery packs and provided aircrew with situational awareness-enhancing imagery of "Blue Force" positioning, Iraqi surface-to-air threats and even schematics showing where the latest SAFIREs had occurred.

'There was an incredible source of talent in the Intel department, and using them for strike planning allowed our aircrew more time to focus on the tactics of the mission. Through the employment of this system, one or two people involved in the strike spent roughly two to four hours preparing for a mission. Although the strike lead was responsible for the product "quality assurance" and attack plan, the rest of the players could show up for the brief and soak in all the essential mission info straight from the kneeboard pack. Once we started conducting close-air support and air interdiction missions, we knew very little about where we would be going or what we would be attacking prior to launching. Therefore, even less time was spent preparing for these missions.'

Aside from strikes on targets in Baghdad, Karbala and a number of other important Iraqi towns in the southern region of the country, airfields, AAA and SAM sites also took a pounding in the first 48 hours of 'Shock and Awe'. CVW-2 D-CAG select Capt Larry Burt, who flew with both CVW-14 and CVW-2 in OIF, succinctly summed up this phase of the campaign;

'We pounded the crap out of the Iraqi Air Force in the first strikes of OIF, hitting his airfields with literally hundreds of TLAMs and JDAM that rendered them inoperable. I think the will of the air force was broken too. As an example of how overwhelmed the Iraqis were, we hit more targets in the first 48 hours of "Shock and Awe" than we did throughout *Desert Storm*. We had done with bombing fixed targets in just two days – there was nothing left on the list to hit, and we had identified literally thousands of targets to bomb going into the war.'

Amongst the prime Iraqi Air Force targets hit in the opening phase of the campaign were the large airfield complexes at H-1, H-2 and H-3, in western Iraq. CVW-2 had

attacked radar sites at these bases in the lead up to OIF, and with the war now underway, a larger strike package was sent to knock out the runways. Strike lead for this mission was Cdr Mark Hubbard of VFA-151;

'Flying with CAG Fox and VFA-137 CO Cdr Walt Stammer, I had briefed for a ten-jet mission, but we lost a Hornet soon after launching with a technical problem and then one of the Tomcats also had a systems failure en route and had to turn back with its wingman in order to maintain section integrity. This caused us to hastily regroup, and resulted in us arriving late for our "gas" and losing our Prowler. I then had to rustle up some F-16CJ support in place of the EA-6B. We finally pressed into western Iraq and headed for the MiG base that we had been tasked with bombing.

'Our mission was to stitch the runways at this airfield and render them inoperable for the duration of OIF. I used to train to attack such targets with six jets carrying 24 unguided dumb bombs, and if you were lucky you might stitch one runway or a taxiway. On this mission, we were all carrying three 2000-lb JDAM apiece, and the five jets that made it to the target stitched the runway every 2000 ft with craters 40 ft in diameter and 20 ft deep. We also knocked out the taxiways and blew up two hardened aircraft shelters, all with just 15 bombs. It would have taken considerably more ordnance, and a lot more jets, to have accomplished this level of destruction in *Desert Storm*.

'During our attack run over the airfield the Iraqis shot six SA-3s and two SA-2s at us. It was so clear that night that it looked like the stars were in the cockpit. CAG Fox was as casual as anything when he saw these things going off, giving us a running commentary on what he could see. "Hey boys, I think they're shooting some SA-3s at us. There's another one, and another one." It was only when they got up to our height that I realised we were in range of them! I then saw an SA-2 go off, and it looked just like an Apollo shot. It was almost enjoyable to watch.'

CVW-5 TCT

Befitting its role as the designated CAS carrier, USS *Kitty Hawk* (CV-63) generated more sorties in support of V Corps' push north into Iraq than against fixed targets in the first few days of OIF. Nevertheless, some elements of CVW-5 did get to hit Time-Critical Targets (TCTs) way north of the Coalition forces in the early stages of the campaign. One of those to fly such a mission was VFA-192's Lt John Allison, who had launched believing that he and his wingman were going to carry out yet another routine CAS sortie;

'My wingman and I flew a mission against a TCT in Baghdad on only the second or third day of the war in response to a request by our E-2 controller to investigate an Al Samoud missile, and its launcher, that had been detected by a UAV. Although we weren't too

Engrossed in his pre-flight cockpit checks, Lt John Allison of VFA-192 prepares to fly an early CAS mission in OIF. Typically, a pilot will take around 45 minutes to methodically work through his cockpit drill, checking circuit breakers, his Martin-Baker SJU-5/A ejection seat and the aircraft's electrical system. Once the Hornet's engines are running, he will go through a series of post-start checks, confirming the proper function of the aircraft's systems, weapons and avionics, prior to giving a ready-to-launch 'thumb's up' to his plane captain. By then the pilot will have completed aligning the Hornet's INS in the carrier-based 'CV' mode, using the ship's INS (SINS) for input. The jet is then finally ready to be unchained and taxied to one of the carrier's four catapults for launching (*Lt John Allison*)

Lt John Allison flew his first OIF mission in this aircraft, Lot XVI F/A-18C BuNo 164905. He snapped this photograph several hours before flying the sortie, with 'Dragon 301' still being armed up by VFA-192's ordnance team. The Hornet has a single 500-lb Mk 82 low drag general purpose bomb on each of its port wing pylons, this unsophisticated weapon proving devastatingly effective in the CAS mission with CVW-5. Note the Hornet's distinctive yellow main gear legs – a tradition upheld by VFA-192 since the 1950s! The 'Golden Dragons' were the only CV-63-based unit to adorn their jets with mission markings, and by the time BuNo 164905 returned to NAF Atsugi on 1 May 2003, it boasted nine LGB, nine JDAM, three Mk 84 and three JSOW silhouettes below its nose modex (*Lt John Allison*)

thrilled about heading into the SuperMEZ in the middle of the day, we nevertheless flew north and started searching for the target. We eventually thought that we had found the missile in the middle of a residential suburb, but we could not positively identify it. Because of its location, we chose not to drop our bombs, and as we came out of the area the whole of Baghdad literally erupted with AAA. We had dropped down quite low in an effort to PID (positively identify) the Al Samoud, so there we were at around 8000 ft in the middle of every AAA and SAM engagement envelope in the world! We quickly got out of there and headed south.

'On the return flight, we happened to stumble across what looked to me like a division's worth of tanks in revetments, all pointing south. These were obviously owned by the Republican Guard, so I quickly flicked through the radio frequencies and ended up talking to a Marine FAC, who agreed to work the area for us. He cleared me "hot", and as I started to roll in on a revetment I spotted a small ammunition bunker right alongside a tank. I dropped my bomb directly into the bunker, which exploded with such ferocity that the secondaries destroyed the tank and created a plume of smoke that topped off at 2000 ft. It looked like a small "nuke" had gone off. I then rolled in on another tank, by which time I could see soldiers shooting at me, so I pumped out my expendables – chaff and flares. I continued to press home my attacks until I was out of fuel and out of expendables, when I finally headed back to the ship.

'Unfortunately, my wingman had missed out on all this action because his jet was suffering from radio problems which prevented him from talking to the FAC – all he could do was orbit overhead. The Iraqis seemed to have placed a considerable number of their tanks in these large reveted areas, which had been hastily created to defend Baghdad.

'My jet was unusually configured on this mission, being armed with a single LGB and two Mk 82 dumb bombs. I got to drop a number of "slicks" during OIF, and these relied on diving attacks for accuracy. We train predominantly with Mk 82s in peacetime due to their relatively cheap cost in relation to an LGB or a JDAM, so mission proficiency with the weapon is not a great issue. The nice thing about a Mk 82 is you can drop the weapon in a dive from high altitude – above the SAM or AAA threat – and as long as your aim is good, with the "diamond" (Auto Computed Release Point) on the target, it is devastatingly accurate.

'When I attacked the tanks in their revetments, the weather was far from ideal for a Mk 82 attack. There was a cloud layer at about 12,000 ft, which had just moved in, so I had to get below it. This in turn meant that I was highlighting myself to the enemy. To compensate for this, I made sure that I kept plenty of speed on the Hornet – I was diving at well over 500 knots –

and pumped out plenty of chaff and flares as I approached the bomb release point. I pulled hard out of my dive and continued to release expendables.

'I made one sighting pass on the target area and two subsequent diving attacks, which saw me put one bomb through the doors of the ammunition bunker and another into a nearby tank. I did not want to drop my LGB as I was not keen to be flying straight and level at below 12,000 ft in such a hostile environment. You can be a lot more aggressive with a dumb bomb, except of course in the dive, where you have to be steady in order to accurately aim the weapon.'

Although the scale of the 'Shock and Awe' offensive had been scaled back to a certain degree, the domination of the skies by the Coalition forces ensured that CAOC's list of fixed targets was worked through in short order. The advent of drastically improved smart weaponry also expedited the neutralising of these targets, which ranged in size from cable repeater vaults in the middle of the desert to multi-storey buildings in downtown Baghdad. On most occasions, JDAM or LGBs were employed to hit these fixed sites, with only a handful of other precision weapons such as AGM-130 and AGM-84 SLAM-ER being brought into play. Indeed, only three of the latter were fired in the entire war, one of them by Lt Cdr Paul Olin of VFA-113;

Three F/A-18Cs from VFA-195 and a solitary yellow-legged VFA-192 machine sit over bow cat one between missions, these aircraft boasting similar war loads. All four have 500-lb GBU-12 LGBs on their outer pylons, with the first three also carrying 500-lb Mk 82 'slicks' (fitted with M904E4 fuses) on the inner pylons. The jet furthest from the camera appears to have a 1000-lb GBU-35(V)2/B JDAM on the inner pylon in place of a dumb bomb (*PH3 Todd Frantom*)

This rare inflight shot of VFA-113's 'Sting 306' (Lot XIV F/A-18C BuNo 164634) was taken on the afternoon of 22 March 2003 as Lt Cdr Paul Olin and his wingman headed for northern Baghdad on CVW-14's sole AGM-84 SLAM-ER mission of OIF. The weapon, clearly visible on the outer port wing pylon of Olin's jet, was successfully guided into a large building (*Lt Cdr Paul Olin*)

VFA-25's 'Fist 413' (Lot XIII F/A-18C BuNo 164266) launches on yet another daylight mission to An Najaf towards the end of the 'Shock and Awe' phase of OIF. Thanks to the employment of precision-guided munitions (PGMs) by strike aircraft that enjoyed total air superiority over Iraq, the Coalition's aerial campaign against fixed targets had achieved its aims by 25 March 2003. VFA-25's XO, Cdr Don Braswell, reflected on how modern warfare had changed as a result of the development of PGMs;

'As we found in OIF, you can expect fixed targets to run out in two or three days in any future conflict. As soon as the bad guys realise that you know how to hit them with PGMs, they work out ways to move and disperse those so-called "fixed" targets. Ten years ago it might have taken four jets and twelve bombs to destroy a fixed target. Since then, naval aviation has evolved through the development of the NITE Hawk targeting pod and smarter PGMs, which we have always had, but we now know how to target them with greater accuracy. We now work on the average of one jet and two targets destroyed, which has forced the enemy to spend a greater effort dispersing his previously fixed targets' (*US Navy*)

'I fired the only SLAM-ER expended by CVW-14 during OIF, targeting a large building in northern Baghdad on the second night of the war. I was fortunate to fly this mission, as I was drafted in as an alternate strike lead at the last minute, being the only one available at that time from VFA-113. We were part of a larger CVW-14 strike package, and my wingman and I were armed exclusively with a single SLAM-ER apiece.

'A fair degree of pre-planning went into the mission, which is typical for the SLAM-ER. It is a superb precision weapon for large targets such as buildings in built-up areas. I had never dropped one before, and it was quite unremarkable to employ, as it falls away from the aircraft before the motor ignites.

'My missile functioned as advertised, although my wingman's weapon malfunctioned and failed to come off the pylon. I duly focused my attention on the solitary SLAM-ER, watching video imagery on my cockpit displays that had been relayed back from the weapon to the AWW-13 data-link pod fitted to the starboard outer wing pylon of my jet. This imagery allowed me to select the desired point of impact for the missile as it entered its terminal phase, and both my wingman and I got excellent video footage of the weapon impacting the targeting cross-hairs on the centre of the building. The results from this mission proved yet again that the SLAM-ER is the long-range precision weapon of choice.

'We were continually asking to use the weapon, but we weren't getting permission from CAOC to employ it. This was almost certainly because overwhelming Coalition air power effectively destroyed most of the pre-planned targets in Iraq in the first 72 hours of the war, and SLAM-ER is a weapon built for attacking pre-planned targets.'

The 'Shock and Awe' phase of OIF had effectively run its course by the time a series of sandstorms of near-biblical proportion rolled into southern Iraq and the NAG on 25 March. From then on, the bulk of Hornet sorties flown in the campaign would be in support of troops on the ground.

SHAPING THE BATTLEFIELD

As mentioned in the previous chapter, the prosecution of OPLAN 1003V called for the ground war to commence after several days of sustained bombing in Iraq. However, this plan was compressed to such a degree that 'G-Day', as the ground invasion was designated, actually preceded 'A-Day'. With mechanised troops from V Corps and the 1st MEF racing into Iraq from Kuwait, hell-bent on reaching Baghdad as quickly as possible, CAOC was forced to switch its focus from destroying fixed targets to conducting Kill box Interdiction Close Air Support (KI/CAS) and Battlefield Air Interdiction (BAI).

Considerable thought had gone into how best to control TACAIR assets in OIF once the ground war got into full swing, with Gen Tommy Franks challenging his war planners to integrate as many air assets as they could into an overall network of 'joint fires' that directly supported ground force commanders. CENTCOM staffers duly came up with the Fire Support Coordination Line (FSCL), which delineated a moving line up to which the 'joint fire' assets – jets, attack helicopters and artillery – were under the control of ground commanders in the field, and beyond which they fell under the jurisdiction of the Joint Force Air Component Commander (JFACC).

Anyone could engage targets beyond the FSCL without coordination with ground units, while targets short of the FSCL had to be be coordinated with the ground commander in whose Area of Responsibility the target resided. The kill box system (detailed below) was used to make the process of updating the FSCL easier, for it allowed the latter to change rapidly without the reissuing of coordinates that defined the line.

This was a radical plan, as traditionally all fixed wing strikers had been controlled exclusively by the JFACC in a time of conflict. Gen Franks placed even more faith in his senior officers on the ground by opting for a 'deep FSCL' once the invasion commenced, this seeing Army or Marine divisional commanders controlling all 'joint fires' out to a range of 100 miles. The value of this extended FSCL was quickly realised when the rapid advances in the south saw friendly forces crossing the 'joint fire' line. Had the TACAIR assets committed to the CAS been controlled by JFACC only, then the potential for friendly fire incidents could have been huge due to AWACS controllers not being fully aware of how far ground forces had advanced.

In an effort to allow JFACC to play its part in the 'deep FCSL' strategy, CENTCOM devised the kill box system. This saw a ground commander split up his area of responsibility into 18.5-mile x 18.5-mile boxes, which he would then declare 'closed' when his troops entered them. Such a system shifted the 'joint fires' responsibility from the JFACC to the

The sandstorms that rolled into the NAG from Iraq made flying conditions extremely hazardous, particularly aboard CV-63, which was positioned the furthest north of the carriers in the Gulf. VFA-192's Lt John Allison remembers;

'The weather turned crappy after the first 72 hours of the war, with sandstorms and thunderstorms arriving in the area at much the same time. I ended up flying through two of these just as it was getting dark, but before I had gone onto NVGs. My jet was hit over a dozen times by lightning, and I could see the bolts clipping the nose of the jet. Then the St Elmo's fire started to dance off the canopy. Amazingly, my jet suffered no damage' (*PH3 Todd Frantom*)

ground commander, thus reducing the chance of fratricide. When a box was declared 'open', JFACC would assume that it was clear of friendly forces and allow Coalition TACAIR assets to prosecute enemy targets.

KI/CAS became a key mission as V Corps and the 1st MEF pushed north, with both forces deliberately manoeuvring around strong points in cities such as An Nasiriyah, Al Kut and An Najaf in an effort to get to Baghdad as quickly as possible in true *Blitzkrieg* style.

Beyond the FSCL, JFACC continued to 'shape the battlefield' in advance of the mechanised troops through CAOC-controlled BAI sorties. Such missions included pre-planned attacks on troop concentrations held in reserve, reveted armour around Baghdad and the selective destruction of bridges so as to stop Republican Guard forces south of the Iraqi capital retreating into the city itself.

As many as 2000 sorties a day were flown as part of the CAS/BAI effort at the height of OIF, with the bulk of these being sent against the forces of the Republican Guard pinned into the Karbala-Baghdad-Al Kut triangle.

Thanks to the Coalition's highly effective combined arms strategy that had seen ground forces working closer with TACAIR than ever before, the 2 Medina, 1 Hammurabi and 5 Baghdad Divisions could not disperse their armoured and mechanised elements for fear of engagement by marauding US Army and Marine Corps M1A1/2 Abrams tanks and helicopter gunships. Concentrating in force was the only defence left open to the Republican Guard, yet this in turn played into the hands of orbiting strike aircraft flying over the battlefield. As Australian defence analyst Carlo Kopp put it;

'What the Coalition campaign strategists set up was a giant three-dimensional combined arms meat grinder, which in a matter of four days placed the Iraqi defenders into an immediate no win situation in which they haemorrhaged irreplaceable land force assets by the hour.'

The only early snag facing the robust implementation of this plan was the rapidly deteriorating weather which arrived in the form of sandstorms five days into the campaign. CV-63's Chief Petty Officer Steven Cole of the vessel's Meteorology and Oceanography Department explained how these conditions occurred;

'The storms were caused by northerly winds which had unsettled sand in the Mesopotamian Valley plain and turned it into fine dust by the time it had reached the NAG. Forecasting in OIF was a challenge because, geographically, the operational area in southern Iraq and the NAG was a closed-in basin surrounded by mountains. It's typically hazy in the Gulf, with seven to eight miles of visibility. On 25 March, visibility went from unrestricted to a quarter-mile in just 15 minutes.'

CVW-2's Capt Mark Fox was airborne at the time the first of the storms arrived in the NAG, and he recalled;

'The weather really got filthy on the 25th – easily as bad as I have ever seen it. When coming back aboard the ship, you would still be struggling to see the deck at three-quarters of a mile. We ended up diverting some guys to shore bases until the storm blew through, leaving our admiral in a great angst about the fact that we were putting guys into the beach. Indeed, we were considering cancelling flight ops.

'Right in the middle of all this, we got a call from the CAOC telling us that they needed us to launch as they thought that there may have been some kind of chemical-biological attack on the Marines somewhere up north. I called the CAOC back and told the Navy captain there that he had to be aware of the fact that I did not think that we would get these jets back aboard ship if they launched in response to this request. He replied that the Marines really needed us. I then went with the "Connie's" captain to see the admiral, and we explained the situation to him, with the rider that if the Marines were asking for TACAIR from CVW-2 then we would give it to them.

'Having just landed back aboard the ship myself from a mission, I was very well aware of how challenging the weather conditions were. He agreed that we should launch the jets, and VFA-151 CO Cdr Mark Hubbard duly led the mission. Several hours later, all the aircraft sortied somehow managed to recover back aboard the carrier in one piece, having supported the Marines as requested.'

A fellow Hornet pilot from VFA-151's sister-unit VFA-137 also revealed his mettle in the middle of the sandstorm, as Capt Fox explained;

'We were the night carrier, so our day would start at 2200 hrs and continue through to the next morning. This meant that the later formations would launch at night and then land in daylight. VFA-137's most junior pilot, Lt(jg) Matt Stoll, sortied in this bad weather on the 25th with my CAG "paddles", Lt Cdr 'Steamer' Raupp – both their jets were armed with JSOW. The weather over the entire Gulf peninsula, covering southern Saudi Arabia, all of Kuwait and out over the NAG, was still really bad. However, we had helped support the Marines in the thick of this dust storm, and with our guys ashore still fighting the war, we continued with our operational tempo.

'Stoll and Raupp rendezvoused with a KC-135 prior to heading into Iraq, plugging into the tanker's wingtip hose and drogue pods. The latter are fitted with take-up reels to help absorb the recoil from the probe when it hits the basket. However, the reel did not work on Stoll's pod, and the recoil wave travelled up the hose and came straight back down again, ripping off the Hornet's probe.

'He had just 5200 lbs of fuel in his tanks, flying over Saudi Arabia, where the weather was zero-zero with dust blowing at ground level.

Kuwait was the same. Stoll ended up doing exactly what he had been instructed to do back in the Hornet Fleet Replacement Squadron – work out where the closest suitable airfield was, which in this case was at King Khallid military city, in Saudi Arabia, build up a radar map of his immediate location and drop the navigational diamond in his HUD on the end of the runway. He would then fly multiple approaches, the first one at 200 ft, the next one at 150 ft, and so on, until he was safely down in one piece.

'These were all self-contained approaches, as King Khallid was closed. Stoll had, however, managed to get hold of someone on the ground, who in turn activated the runway lights. Aside from this, the only help he got was from the KC-135 crew he had rendezvoused with for fuel. They fed him data on the layout of the airfield, and told him that there were no obstructions to the west. Being a "nugget", Stoll was literally too young to be scared! He landed at King Khallid with 600 lbs of fuel left, which would have given him less than five minutes of flying time in the Hornet.

'Stoll had kept his JSOW on the jet throughout this episode, as I had personally instructed all my crews not to jettison ordnance unless it was a dire emergency – which this was, although he was too inexperienced to realise it! Anxious to get back to the ship as quickly as he could, Stoll eventually got some "gas", jumped back into his jet and blasted off to come back to the "Connie". Of course by the time he got back over the carrier our flying day had been completed, so he had to trap aboard the day carrier, *Lincoln*. God bless them, the Hornet guys on CVN-72 fixed the aeroplane's probe and Stoll came back to us later that day with a fully mission-capable jet! Indeed, it flew in the first wave that night.

'When I quizzed Stoll as to why he had done what he did, he simply replied, without bravado, that he had a game plan and he was "working it"! He handled the whole event as well as a veteran Hornet pilot with 3000 hours on the jet. I e-mailed a report of this episode to Fifth Fleet Commander Adm Tim Keating, who replied that it "made his heart soar like an eagle"! It made my heart soar too once it started beating again.'

CVW-14 also got the call to launch aircraft in the midst of the sandstorms on 25 March, and one of those pilots who battled the elements was the CO of VFA-113, Cdr Bill Dooris. He wrote about his experiences in the following entry from his OIF combat diary;

'Last night was one of the most challenging I've ever had. It was clearly a night that we would have cancelled flight ops had we not been at war. Lightning was striking all around the ship, and it was solid clouds from 2000 ft to 35,000 ft, which meant nowhere to rendezvous with your wingman – in this case "Lo Roller". I could tell he was VERY nervous going into the flight, not comfortable at all with how low we could get on gas, with nowhere else to land but back at the ship. On top of that CAG Albright was also participating in the flight, and he told us at the briefing, "This will be the hardest flight of your lives. The weather conditions make this extremely difficult, but the guys on the ground are getting killed and they need us".

'The sand kicked up by very high winds on the beach had made the visibility zero in the region, stopping the USAF from flying. The Navy was asked to take up the slack by adding some more sorties to the flight schedule. We pressed on in the worse conditions I have ever seen.

'We planned to have a F/A-18E tanker drag us into the country, but we were worried about climbing up through the clouds with three jets in tight formation. In addition, icing up of the wings would be a problem if we climbed too slowly. Several flights had returned from Iraq saying they could not get close enough to their lead aircraft to keep him in sight in the clouds.

'Now imagine this. Flying ten feet away from another jet, both of which are moving at 400 mph, four miles above the earth. This we do every day. But then you lose sight of each other. Turn the wrong way and you will collide. So we have a plan should this occur. The wingman turns away from the leader and takes a two-mile trail on him until you break out of the clouds.

Although further south than CV-63, CVN-72 was also forced to operate in the poor weather that blighted the NAG from 25 March 2003. Units operating from shore bases in the region were effectively grounded during this period, but the carriers continued to generate sorties as directed by CAOC (*US Navy*)

'Lt Cdr James "Marvin" Haigler, flying my tanker, launched and told me that there was no clear air above the ship, and he was proceeding into Iraq to find clear air to meet us. I launched and found that he was 14 miles away, so I started a slow catch up with him. My wingman had had to vacate his jet on the flight deck and jump into another one due to an equipment failure with his original machine, and I was told that his launch would be delayed by 20 minutes. This was usually not a big deal, except tonight there was nowhere to wait for him without burning lots of extra gas (this mission was going to be close on fuel anyway) or icing up the jet. We decided that I could not wait for him, and would go into Iraq with the armed tanker as my wingman instead. Although "Marvin" had no bombs, he did have air-to-air missiles, so he could watch my tail as I dropped my bombs.

'As we climbed, me still running him down, completely unable to see the nose of my jet, St Elmo's fire – a static electricity discharge that lights up the cockpit – appeared on the windscreen as if it were cracking from a rock thrown at it. And because it was night, it was blinding every time it flashed (every two seconds). You can imagine what an electrical storm does to your radios too – tons of static, making them almost inaudible.

'As we passed through 28,000 ft, with no stars yet in sight (still very much in the "goo"), I was at the one-mile point right behind my tanker, whose pilot desperately needed to lighten his fuel load so that he could climb higher and get out of the icing. At half-a-mile I still could not see him, and was scanning airspeed closure and altitude difference so as to not run into, or past, him. At 0.3 miles I started to see the "pops" of his anti-collision lights and switched to guns tracking, as it would display out feet instead of miles. At 2400 ft I started to see his lights. With 20 knots of closure, I tried to slowly creep up on him.

'This whole time we had been switching frequencies, listening out for reports of clear air, and someone who could use our ordnance to put on their enemies' heads – we had switched frequencies nearly eight times. Each time we did this, the tanker pilot had to tell me the frequency because I couldn't look at my "freq" list. If I had looked at anything but him, I would have lost sight of the tanker, and then possibly collided with it. I did, however, quickly look at the DDI (Data Display Indicator) showing the outside temperature to see if we were in icing conditions. I had this displayed on the DDI which usually featured my map, so I had no idea of whether we were in Iraq yet or not, and if I should have be worrying about SAMs.

'After checking the DDI for no more than two seconds, I looked through the HUD to discover that I had built up my closure rate to such a degree that I was about to run into my tanker. I easily missed him by dropping down and to the right, still trying to stay close enough to see him in the thick clouds. I also pulled my power back to stop the rate of closure, but this in turn caused my jet to slide away from the tanker, and I lost sight of it for a second. I jammed the power up for one to two seconds, before pulling it back to idle and then finally resetting it in mid range. Now I could see him again, but I couldn't stop from sliding past him on his right. With the tanker above and behind me to the left, I was going to have to be very lucky – or damn good – to save this one.

'Visibility was two wingspans (100 ft). I had a bail out plan, but didn't want to have to rejoin. "'Marvin', go to 'burner NOW". This not only put him out in front of me, it also lit up the tanker so I could see him more easily. This was just what I needed, and I slid in and tucked under his right wing. Five minutes later we were looking better, and after a further five minutes of stabbing at the refuelling basket, I was in and taking fuel. We were so high and slow that I needed to crack 'burner to stay in the basket.

'Soon after I was finished, we popped into clear air, with the beautiful stars above us and solid clouds below. As I took the lead of the flight, I started looking for clearance to drop my ordnance – JDAM – on my back-up target. We had been through four "freqs" where no one wanted to use us. It turned out that our back-up target area had friendlies in it and was closed, but the controller was working on opening it. Then my world started to go bad fast.

'Two red Bleed Air lights illuminated on my console, indicating a very hot air leak – usually the precursor to a fire in the engine bay. Just as quickly, the automatic valves shut off the leak and the lights went out. But now I had no oxygen, and at the high altitudes we were at, I would not last more than 30 seconds. I activated the back-up oxygen, which was designed to last long enough to allow me to do a rapid descent to lower altitudes. But this was something that the threat, the weather and the fuel would not allow me to do.

'The following scenario quickly posed itself – I would be forced to descend to stay conscious, but then if I wasn't downed by missiles or AAA, I would run out of fuel and have to eject. This entire thought process took ten seconds. I was seriously up a creek. The only thing I could try was to reset the Bleed Air valves – something definitely against NATOPS, but required to survive. It worked, and my normal oxygen was restored.

'I'll be damned if I went through all this effort to turnaround 30 miles prior to the target and not drop. Besides, getting rid of extra drag and weight would help me arrive home safe.

'As I was concentrating on checking the proper coordinates and settings for the bomb, I looked through the HUD to find myself 20 degrees nose high in a 30-degree left bank, turning into my wingman at a very slow airspeed. I kicked myself for not correctly prioritising. Twenty seconds prior to dropping the JDAM, I was panicked that I would not get them off, but all went smoothly. Bombs away, hard turn out away from the threat and off toward "mother" (the ship). One hour later, after a very challenging return tanking and difficult approach through rain and wind shears on final, I caught the three wire at 0100 hrs.'

BUDDY-LASING FOR VS-38

Just hours prior to the arrival of the sandstorms in the NAG, history had been made when an S-3B of VS-38, assigned to CVW-2, fired an AGM-65E Maverick missile at Saddam's 6000-ton presidential yacht, the *Al Mansur*, sat at anchor in Basra harbour. This was the first time that a Viking had employed such a weapon in combat in 30 years of fleet service, and VFA-151's Lt Cdr Ron Candiloro provided the targeting guidance for the Maverick with the integral laser rangefinder housed in the AAS-38B FLIR pod affixed to his jet. His participation in this historic mission was very much a last-minute thing, as he explained to the author;

'CVW-2 operated like most other air wings in that we had our chosen "players", who were scheduled for the event. Jets don't always work as they should 100 per cent of the time, so you would always have a spare aircraft built into the mission plan. Its pilot would conduct the full brief and strap into the jet on the deck. On 25 March 2003, when I manned the spare, there was an ordnance screw up and I had to launch with no weapons on my jet other than the basic air-to-air load-out. I was basically going to be little more than a place filler if I launched.

'With the exception of the Prowler, single tactical jets are not allowed to fly by themselves into country, so should I be called on, my job now was to act as a wingman or strike lead for a Hornet with bombs. I was sitting on the back of carrier, and everybody said that they were good to go over the intercom, so I thought that they would just taxi me forward and shut me down, as that was what usually happened when the spare was not required. As I was being marshalled towards the catapult, last in line for the launch cycle, I got a call from the ship's central watch, which coordinates everything happening on the deck. They told me that I was to launch, join up with another jet and head into Iraq.

'It turned out that I had been paired up with an S-3 that had been tasked with attacking Saddam's yacht, anchored in Basra harbour. My job was to put laser energy on the vessel and the S-3 was going to shoot its single laser Maverick at its bridge area – we had received reports that its extensive radio suite was being used for battlefield communications. Fortunately for me, I had happened to see a photo

AGM-65E laser Maverick-armed S-3B BuNo 160589 of VS-38 unfold's its wings aboard CV-64 on 3 February 2003. This combination made the headlines seven weeks later, on 25 March, when the following report appeared in a San Diego newspaper;

'The "Red Griffins" of Sea Control Squadron 38 made a bit of history early yesterday, demonstrating that they really are fighters, not just gas station attendants. A crew from the North Island Naval Air Station-based S-3B squadron fired a laser-guided Maverick missile to destroy a "significant naval target" in the Tigris River near Basra – about 60 miles inland – after launching from the aircraft carrier *Constellation*.

'It was the first time that the versatile S-3B had been sent on a "time-critical", overland attack in the Viking's 30 years of Navy service, and the first time one had fired a laser-guided weapon in combat. The mission was flown by Lt Cdr Richard McGrath, with Lt Cdr Carlos Sardiello directing the mission as tactical control officer, and Lt Michael Harvey handling communications, navigation and weapons. The S-3B has been used mostly as a tanker since hostilities broke out. "This was an excellent example of the Navy being able to do things at very short notice, and the teamwork that we exhibit", McGrath said. Hornet pilot Lt Cdr Ron Candiloro provided the laser illumination, and he said that he considered it a chance to repay the S-3s for their support. "These guys are the unsung heroes of the air wing. They provide gas for us and don't get a lot of glory"' (*US Navy*)

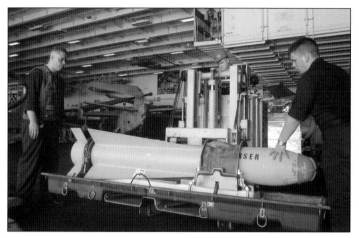

The venerable AGM-65E laser Maverick proved an extremely effective weapon in OIF, being used extensively in both urban and battlefield CAS missions following on from its success in Kosovo in 1999 during Operation *Allied Force* and then in Afghanistan in Operation *Enduring Freedom* in 2001-02. This particular AGM-65E is being uncrated in the hangar bay of CV-64 prior to being loaded onto an Aero-12C skid and taken up to the flight deck. Capt Larry Burt got to use Mavericks upon his return to CVW-2 in the final days of OIF;

'We fired between four and six hollow-warhead laser Mavericks in Baghdad right at the end of the war, as this was our urban CAS weapon of choice. Maverick is popular in built up areas because its warhead becomes inert if guidance of the weapon is lost for any reason. This greatly reduces the risk of collateral damage. Therefore, it is either guiding onto the target as directed by the laser seeker or it is a safe weapon' (*US Navy*)

of the yacht in the ready room just before I walked to my jet. I had studied the shot long enough to pick out its distinguishing features, so once we got into the target area I had no problem identifying the vessel. We performed a few dummy runs on the yacht, and then I successfully guided the Maverick into the target. This was the first time that the yacht had been attacked

'We approached the vessel from medium altitude, which placed us above the known IADS threat for the area, but was still a little lower than I was comfortable with. It was a daytime mission fairly close to the NAG, so I felt that if I was hit and my jet did not explode immediately, I could at least limp to the water before ejecting.

'I was not involved in the planning for this mission at any stage. Indeed, the Hornet pilot who had conducted the pre-flight brief for this sortie, and who was slated to lase for the S-3, ended up being tasked with another mission minutes before launching!'

The presidential yacht remained a target for TACAIR aircraft for much of the campaign, with crews from CVW-14 also attacking it, including VFA-25 XO Cdr Don Braswell;

'I dropped two LGBs on Saddam's yacht, but when I came back and was told that twelve other bombs had also been put into the vessel, I wished I had dropped my ordnance on another target. We were never going to sink it the size it was, and it would have taken less than 14 bombs to disable it. Although it was a big white ship, there were so many other vessels on the pier, you actually had to count ships so as to find the yacht. My controller told me to spot a bridge first, and then go back three ships from there. He then said, "Do you see vessel that is angled off?", and I replied "Yes I do". "It's not that one", he continued, "but the one next to it"! Was the yacht being used as a military asset? I don't know, and it was not my call. It did, however, have sufficient radio equipment to be used as a communications platform.'

A drastic improvement in the weather from 27 March onwards saw carrier sortie rates increase even more as Navy TACAIR assets set about attacking Republican Guard divisions in the Karbala-Baghdad-Al Kut triangle, as well as countering pockets of Iraqi Army and Fedayeen resistance in bypassed towns south of the FSCL. Capt Larry Burt, who, uniquely, flew with both CVW-14 and CVW-2 in OIF, performed over 20 KI/CAS and BAI missions in the critical phase of the war between 26 March and 5 April;

'For most of the campaign we were either fragged for KI/CAS or BAI, working directly with troops on the ground. When performing the latter mission, you would typically operate with J-STARs and an E-3 AWACS, which were in turn working through the CAOC. They also had control of UAVs, and the on-the-spot intelligence that they provided. You would be sent to a certain area and instructed to find something to bomb, or they

would locate a target for you and simply relay its coordinates, along with the instruction to go and hit it.

'If you were fragged for KI/CAS, soon after launching you would check in with an E-2 controller, who was in turn talking to "Warhawk" – running the "Black" target list for the Army and Marines – at CAOC. The E-2 guy would be working your tasking for you as you headed north, checking whether the ground forces had targets for you, or whether they could open up kill boxes behind their FSCL if no CAS targets were available. In a perfect world, by the time we checked in again with the E-2 once in Iraq, he would simply hand us over to a FAC or a FAC(A), and we would go and drop our ordnance.

'The FACs that were rolling with the Army did not have all the "toys" that their SOF equivalents were able to employ. They had to provide more talk-on CAS as a result. They would say something like, "We are rolling down this road, and do you see the bend up ahead of us? We are taking fire from mortars in the nearby treeline. Do you see the treeline? Put a bomb into the treeline". I would reply in the affirmative and duly bomb the treeline. I had this happen to me on a couple of occasions, and both times I could not physically see the enemy. You would simply put the bomb where you thought the FAC wanted it. This was very nerve-wracking, because you were so paranoid about putting a bomb on "friendlies" or civilians down there.

'On many of these CAS missions, I found myself flying over downtown Karbala, or a suburb of Baghdad, while my FAC tried to talk my eyes onto a certain tree in an area where there were trees all over the place! Or maybe he wanted me to hit a ditch next to a field, when there were ditches and fields as far as you could see. When faced with such requests, typically, I would go down and try and get a better look at the target area, and by doing so I then became the target!

'Such missions were tough, as you were only ever 90 per cent sure that the target the FAC was describing was the one you were indeed attacking. The experiences of this conflict have shown that we have to get better at picking out where the "friendlies" are in an urban battlefield. The technology is there to allow us to do it, but we must now implement it.'

FLIR AND LGBs

Over 5000 of the 5300 bombs dropped by Navy Hornet and Tomcat crews in OIF were precision-guided. In the 'Shock and Awe' phase of the

VFA-25's CO jet (Lot XIV F/A-18C BuNo 164635) has been attached to waist cat four in preparation for launch on 5 April 2003. Delivered to the Navy in October 1991, this aircraft was immediately issued to VFA-25 as part of the unit's re-equipment with the latest Hornet variant. The squadron had previously traded its Lot XI F/A-18Cs to VFA-192 in the 'Great Air Wing SwapEx' in August 1991, which had seen CVW-5 move from USS *Midway* (CV-41) to USS *Independence* (CV-62). VFA-25 duly brought VFA-192's old Lot VIII F/A-18As back to Lemoore, and these were quickly replaced with the Lot XIV F/A-18Cs that the unit continues to fly today. 'Fist 401' is armed with 500-lb GBU-12 bombs beneath each wing, VFA-25 dropping no fewer than 171 of these LGBs in OIF – more than any other TACAIR squadron in CVW-14. Unit XO Cdr Don Braswell expended a number of LGBs during the campaign;

'We primarily hit armour and military vehicles, or anything that looked like it might be able to move around. We were told not to bomb buildings, as they would just have to be rebuilt after the war – this remained a constant theme throughout the conflict. Statistically at least, we hit 90 per cent of the targets we aimed at, but just how many of those tanks and APCs we bombed were truly operable and ready to go and attack American troops we will never know. We do know, however, that they were military targets which fell within the strict collateral damage restraints that we operated in during OIF' (*US Navy*)

The Lockheed Martin AAS-38B NITE Hawk pod was the F/A-18's primary targeting sensor in OIF, this particular example being carried by an F/A-18E of VFA-115 (*VFA-115*)

Below
VFA-25's Lt Anton Orr checks the fuse wiring on a GBU-12 attached to the inner port wing pylon of his jet (*US Navy*)

Bottom
'Switch 307' (Lot XV F/A-18C BuNo 164739) of VFA-151 boasts a DCA weapons configuration (*US Navy*)

campaign, GPS-guided J-weapons such as JDAM and JSOW had been the preferred munitions of choice. However, with the list of fixed targets having been exhausted in less than 72 hours, and ground forces rolling north, the weaponry 'spotlight' shifted to the laser-guided bomb (LGB), thanks to its flexibility.

The key to the successful employment of LGBs is accurate targeting from laser designators either carried in bolt-on pods fitted to Navy TACAIR types such as the F/A-18 and F-14, in mast-mounted sites on combat helicopters such as the OH-58 or AH-64, or hand-held by FACs on the ground. The Hornet's pod is the Lockheed Martin AAS-38B NITE (Navigational Infra-red Targeting Equipment) Hawk FLIR-LTD/R (Forward-Looking Infra-Red Laser Target Designator/Ranger), which has been in fleet service since January 1993.

A somewhat temperamental piece of equipment, the NITE Hawk pod has both its champions and its detractors in the light strike community. Regardless of personal opinion, the pod was the primary targeting tool for Navy Hornets in OIF, and pilots either lived with its limitations as best they could, or found alternative ways to guide their bombs, as Capt Burt related to the author;

'The FLIR pod on the Hornet was generally reliable, and I only suffered one failure. However, I did read about a number of FLIR head

"tumbles" while looking through the CTF-50 mission reports aboard the *Lincoln*. I am not a fan of the NITE Hawk FLIR pod both in terms of its reliability and capability. Therefore, if I was told that there was a Tomcat crew working a FAC(A) or SCAR (Strike Coordination Attack and Reconnaissance) mission nearby, I would operate with them. I would fly over to where they were, check in with them and, for the most part, they would "talk my eyes" onto the target.

'It must be said that the Tomcat's LANTIRN pod is not that much better than the NITE Hawk, despite the fact that it makes better TV pictures for post-mission BHA. That is more a function of how the LANTIRN's video picture is recorded. In the Hornet, we have cameras in the cockpit that really don't adapt to the environment very well, resulting in washed-out pictures. The LANTIRN system records its pictures digitally within the optical processor, rather than simply recording what the display physically shows the pilot. There-

fore, what you see on our mission tapes is drastically inferior to the pod picture shown in the cockpit.

'Where the FAC(A) crew come into their own is by telling me that the speck that I can see on my pod is a tank, despite the fact that I cannot physically distinguish this myself, either with my naked eye or with my sensors. With this confirmation, I can hit the target just as easy with the NITE Hawk as I can with the LANTIRN. The FAC(A) guys are a boon for us single-seat TACAIR pilots in a CAS scenario, as they are sitting up there running the battle-

field by identifying targets using binoculars and the various other sensors that they can bring into play. Their ability to loiter over the target area also helps them build up a picture of what is happening on the ground.'

Although Tomcat FAC(A) crews were operating all over Iraq, their numbers were limited due to the fact that just 56 F-14s were committed to OIF, versus 250 Hornets. In the main, F/A-18 pilots either self- or buddy-lased with the NITE Hawk pod, as Capt Burt explained;

'I lased for my wingman on four or five occasions, either because he could not see the target or his jet had a FLIR problem. This was fairly straightforward as long as you had the correct laser codes dialled in to the weapons computer. I would call him in close to my jet and tell him "Stand by to drop". His bomb was configured in a manual mode, and he would simply pickle the weapon when I told him to. The laser "basket" from the NITE Hawk is quite large – it does not have to be a precise point – and I would then manually fire my designator at the target and guide the LGB in. I was fortunate enough to achieve hits every time I did this in OIF, the bombs landing exactly where I was aiming.

'My wingman and I would usually make our first pass over the target area at 15,000 ft in an effort to spot what the FACs were trying to talk us onto. If that didn't work, I would come back at 10,000 ft, with my wing-

man stepped up looking through my aircraft at 12,000 ft. His primary job was to look for SAMs and MANPADS coming up at us, leaving me to concentrate on trying to find the target. If I still couldn't locate it, we would come back around at 5000 ft and keep on working down until I found it. Admittedly, from a tactics perspective, making numerous passes at ever lower altitudes is stupid, but when your troops are under fire on the ground, screaming for your help, you really don't have much

Three GBU-12s are wheeled towards a VFA-137 jet (out of shot) in late March 2003. No fewer than 423 500-lb LGBs were expended by CVW-2 during OIF (as well as four in OSW) (*US Navy*)

A section of VFA-113 jets go in search of targets in the Karbala-Baghdad-Al Kut triangle on 28 March 2003. Both Hornets are identically configured, with a GBU-12 on the outer port wing pylon and two 500-lb Mk 82 'slicks' on a single BRU-33 Canted Vertical Ejector Rack attached to the starboard outer pylon. Note that the trailing jet is carrying three external tanks. VFA-113 dropped the most ordnance of the four TACAIR units assigned to CVW-14 in OIF, expending 18 GBU-31s, 87 GBU-35s, 132 GBU-12s, four GBU-16s, one SLAM-ER, 38 JSOW and 29 'others' ('slick' bombs and laser Mavericks) (*US Navy*)

choice. We would adopt similar tactics at night too, dropping down to an altitude where your FLIR pod could help you identify the target.

'My most memorable buddy-lasing mission was flown from the *Lincoln* with a brand new nugget who had joined his squadron maybe a month before the war had started – I don't know how they had got him out there! I dragged this guy north to Baghdad, and he couldn't find the target. I was literally carrying this guy around, and at one point he even lost sight of me. Having said that, he was doing a good job lookout-wise, as we were getting heavily shot at, and he kept up a running commentary on where the bullets were coming from. I ended up buddy-lasing his bombs into the target, as there was no way he going to find it, and by now the FAC was being shot at too. We left the area and returned to the ship, and by the time I got back on deck my knees were shaking – this was an intense mission, and I was exhausted. My wingman, by contrast, "bee-bopped" into the ready room as if what we had just experienced was a routine sortie for a naval aviator!'

Capt Burt also commented on the successful implementation of Gen Franks' 'deep FSCL' strategy, which allowed ground forces to push rapidly northwards into Iraq;

'The forces on the ground bypassed a lot of the Iraqi Army in their drive on Baghdad. The Marines proved particularly adept at this, and they usually avoided getting anchored down in frontal assaults on troop concentrations. They would leave areas open behind their frontline into which we flew in search of targets to attack. Anything forward of the FSCL we could attack independently once assigned an open kill box by our controller – it had to be free of SOF for it to be declared open. Kill boxes behind the FSCL had to be worked through a ground FAC, and he controlled what was to be hit inside those boxes.

'The Army kept on moving its FSCL northwards, bypassing large numbers of Iraqi troops and closing a lot of kill boxes that we had previously been using. This prevented us from bombing targets that remained in these areas because the Army had no FACs available to tell us what we could and couldn't hit. The Marines, however, kept the FSCL closer to its troops, and when they bypassed Iraqi forces they would keep the kill boxes open.

'We always knew that if V Corps had nothing for you, you could roll over to the Marine controllers and they would direct you south to one of their kill boxes between Basra and Al Amarah – there were pockets of resistance in these areas until war's end. The Marines had bypassed eastern Iraq, having taken An Nasiriyah and then headed directly north to Al Kut. With the British kept busy dealing with Basra, this left everything north of the city up to Al Kut wide open, and TACAIR was given the job of pounding bypassed troops and armour in this region.'

GO FOR YOUR GUN

Although viewed as a weapon of last resort, the Hornet's 20 mm M61A1 Vulcan cannon proved its worth over the battlefield on more than one occasion. VFA-151 CO Cdr Mark Hubbard was amongst the first pilots in CVW-2 to fire his gun in anger;

'I got to do some high-angle strafing at night against some vehicles that were parked up in a garrison south of Baghdad. The FAC we were working with had initially asked us to bomb some tanks that he had spotted nearby, which he believed were being brought together for a counter-attack on the V Corps frontline. He gave us some solid coordinates and we hit the target with our JDAMs, followed by our LGBs. He then spotted the vehicles and asked us to strafe them. My wingman and I had incendiary rounds loaded into our magazines, and these would set wood and fabric alight when they hit.

'I commenced my attack by rolling in at 15,000 ft, strafing from 12,000 ft and then levelling out at 10,000 ft. My dive angle was between 45 and 60 degrees, and as long as you had the speed, you could hit the target with great accuracy even from that height. We made four passes, with our aim getting better and better and our FAC getting progressively more excited with every run. He told us that he had a "bunch of Iraqi vehicles on fire – nice work!" We took it in turns to attack, my wingman holding off and performing high cover while I strafed, and I then gave the same coverage to him when he attacked.

'Just as he began to make his first attacking run, my wingman informed me that he had never fired the gun before, even in training! He told me that he could not get any gun symbology on his HUD, so I talked him through it. On his third roll in I asked him how many rounds he had left. He told me that he had about 390 – the magazine carries 570! I asked him if he had the gun set up in single fire mode, and he replied that he was worried about burning the barrels out! I told him that there were not enough rounds in the magazine to do this, and if he kept the gun button pressed down he would run out of shells in about six seconds anyway. He all but emptied his magazine on his next pass.'

Not all pilots favoured using the cannon, with VFA-25's Cdr Don Braswell explaining his reservations about the weapon to the author;

'Strafing was only done as a last resort if the guy on the ground was screaming for assistance and you had no other ordnance left. The gun is hard to load, slows the turnaround of the jet between missions, is difficult to clean and is not 100 per cent reliable. If a round jams when it is being fired, for example, the maintenance guys will have to spend several hours stripping the weapon in order to remove the shell, possibly causing the aircraft to be scrubbed from a mission.'

Despite the reservations expressed by Cdr Braswell, most pilots were tempted to use the gun, particularly when faced with an abundance of targets in a seemingly deserted kill box. VFA-192's Lt John Allison encountered just such a scenario;

'On one of my KI/CAS missions in late March, my wingman and I had just launched when we were told to go and investigate what was believed to be a terrorist training camp near the Iranian border. When we arrived over the target area, we found a number of Al Samoud missiles, and their

'Ordies' from VFA-137 load a belt of 20 mm high explosive incendiary ammunition into the magazine of an F/A-18C aboard CV-64 on 21 March 2003. Some 570 rounds can be carried in the magazine, which feeds the M61A1 Vulcan cannon at a rate of 6000 rounds per minute (*US Navy*)

This weapon has been removed from a VFA-137 jet so that routine maintenance can be carried out on the barrels of the rotary cannon. Although a highly accurate weapon, the M61A1 can be labour intensive, and is prone to jamming (*US Navy*)

'Mace 203' (Lot XII F/A-18C BuNo 164010) departs waist cat four at the start of another KI/CAS mission from CV-63 in early April 2003. VFA-27 had all but dispensed with AAMs by this stage of the war, arming BuNo 164010 with just a single AIM-9M on its port wingtip rail (out of shot). The obligatory GBU-12 is carried on the starboard outer wing pylon, while the port outer pylon boasts a single BRU-33 Canted Vertical Ejector Rack, complete with two 500-lb Mk 82 'slicks' (*PH3 Todd Frantom*)

Some Hornets units operating in the NAG went to a three-tank fit in an effort to increase their loiter time over the battlefield as the frontline moved progressively northwards away from the Gulf. 'Fist 411' (Lot XIV F/A-18C BuNo 164645) also carries a smaller pod on its outer starboard pylon. This is possibly an AWW-13 data link pod (*US Navy*)

launchers, in revetments within the camp compound. We attacked these at dusk, and I saw rockets cooking off and firing horizontally across the ground just seconds after our LGBs had impacted the revetments.

'Having used all our bombs, we then contemplated going down and strafing some nearby buildings which had been covered with camouflage netting to hide equipment. However, it was rapidly getting darker, and although there seemed to be no AAA threat, we decided that it was not a wise move. We therefore called in a second section of Hornets some ten minutes behind us to bomb the buildings, and they in turn told the AWACS that there was a whole lot more military equipment in the camp. Two F-15E Strike Eagles were then given the task of finishing off what we had started.'

EXTENDING THE RANGE

As ground forces moved further north into Iraq, the 'legacy' Hornet's age old problem of limited range became more exacerbated the closer V Corps and the 1st MEF got to Baghdad. TACAIR assets had initially struggled with a paucity of tanker support in the 'Shock and Awe' phase of OIF, and as the campaign developed, the F/A-18's modest loiter time over the battlefield started to have a detrimental affect on the levels of support that Navy squadrons could offer the troops on the ground.

All three air wings in the NAG looked at ways to solve this problem, and various strategies were implemented. VFA-113's Lt Cdr Paul Olin recalls;

'In an effort to combat the F/A-18C's modest range, we switched from carrying two to three external tanks once we got more involved in flying KI/CAS missions. This was unusual for a west coast squadron, although east coast Hornet units regularly fly in this configuration. Such a fit bought us more loiter time, particularly when operating over Karbala and Baghdad. An additional tank gave us an extra 30 to 40 minutes on station, which became very useful as the targets began to run out. On the downside, the jets felt heavier and more lethargic in this configuration – to make matters worse, we were flying Lot XIV aircraft, which were the heaviest Hornets still fitted with the old F404 engines.'

Aside from increasing the number of external tanks fitted to their jets, CVN-72's two F/A-18C units looked to fellow CVW-14 TACAIR squadron VFA-115, flying the F/A-18E, to help solve their range problems, as Cdr Don Braswell explains;

'In my opinion, the Super Hornet's greatest contribution to CVW-14's warfighting ability in OIF was when it was configured with four tanks and a buddy refuelling store. Normally, we would have to go to a "big wing" tanker some 45 minutes' flying time away in order to get 8000 lbs of fuel, before heading to Baghdad. On the return leg, you would hit another USAF tanker for a further 8000 lbs of gas. This resulted in an overall mission time of three hours and forty-five minutes, and cost 16,000 lbs of fuel to put two bombs per jet on a target.

'When operating with Super Hornet tankers, they would launch with us strikers and follow us in-country. We only needed to take 6000 lbs of fuel en route because we could tank at higher altitudes, rather than wasting fuel descending to a "big wing" tanker and then having to climb back up to our previous cruising height. Being a tactical tanker, the Super Hornet ended up closer to the target with you, meaning that you in turn arrived on station with more fuel, thus increasing your loiter time.

'CVW-14 accomplished a lot more in OIF thanks to the tanking ability of the Super Hornet. The aircraft proved so capable in this mission that we stopped using the "big wing" USAF tankers about a week into the campaign, relying exclusively on F/A-18Es heading into Iraq and S-3s coming back.

'Typically, on an OIF mission to Baghdad, a section of two Hornets would be dragged north by a single Super Hornet tanker, and we would take it in turns to take fuel from him en route to the target. Some 45 minutes from Baghdad we would kick him off, as he had to return to the ship within a 90-minute cycle. Prior to his departure, we would have taken on around 6000 lbs of fuel each, so we were now fully topped off. Having dropped our bombs, we headed back south from the target and rendezvoused with a

CVW-14's solution to its tanker problem was solved by configuring four of VFA-115's Super Hornets in a permanent 'five-wet' fit. 'Talon 210' (Block XXIII F/A-18E BuNo 165789) was one of those converted into a tactical tanker. Laden down with two 480-US gal FPU-11 external fuel tanks under each wing and an Aero D704 Aerial Refueling Store on the SUU-78 centreline pylon, the aircraft is in tension, ready for launching from CVN-72's bow cat one. VFA-115 was more than prepared for this new mission, as the following entry from its cruise report clearly indicated;

'VFA-115 also performed the less glamorous, but no less important, role of aerial tanking. This mission was thrust upon the unit when it became clear that the air war would be hampered by a lack of airborne tankers. Providing organic air wing tanking for CVW-14, the "Eagles" began flying 18-20 refuelling sorties a day on top of its continuing cycle of strike missions. Since one Super Hornet tanker could provide fuel to two strike aircraft, the squadron's efforts, in conjunction with the S-3Bs of VS-35, facilitated about 40 sorties per day from CVN-72. By war's end VFA-115 had passed 2.3 million lbs of fuel, generating more than 430 extra combat sorties' (*VFA-115*)

With no Super Hornets available, CVW-2 relied on a combination of S-3Bs and Hornets configured with three tanks in order to get around its loiter time issues with the F/A-18C. Here, 'Switch 310' (BuNo 164719) takes on fuel from VS-38's 'Griffin 701' (BuNo 160126). The latter jet was passed on to CVW-5's VS-21 when CV-64 chopped out of the NAG, VS-38 in turn receiving BuNo 160572, which was virtually out of flying hours. The unit also traded two other low-time S-3s with CVW-11's VS-29, being given time-expired jets in return (*VFA-151*)

Navy light strike's sole combat fatality in OIF was VFA-195's Lt Nathan White, whose Hornet was downed by a PAC-3 Patriot missile on the night of 2 April 2003 during a KI/CAS mission in support of the US Army's 3rd Infantry Division. The shattered F/A-18C crashed into a lake in an Iraqi Air Force bombing range near Karbala, and its location subsequently hindered efforts made by the US Army's TRAP (Tactical Recovery of Aircraft and Personnel) team to retrieve Lt White's body. The pilot's remains were eventually discovered in the lake on 12 April, and he was buried with full military honours in the Arlington National Cemetery 12 days later (*Nathan White Family Archive*)

S-3 from VS-35, which would give us a squirt of "gas" prior to us landing back aboard the carrier.'

CVW-2 could not fall back on the Super Hornet tanker option, having instead to rely on "big wing" tankers and tactical 'gas' from VS-38's eight S-3s embarked in the 'Connie'. VFA-151's Lt Cdr Ron Candiloro fully appreciated the effort made by the Viking unit – which was on its last cruise prior to disestablishment – to get the trio of Hornet units over the battlefield;

'When executing our routine KI/CAS missions, we were limited by our time on station. Initially, we were also hampered by our USAF tankers not being allowed into Iraq. CVW-2 got around this during the "Shock and Awe" phase of OIF by performing four or five large strike missions on fixed targets without external tanker support. These sorties could only be flown if every S-3 that was on the flight plan made it to the correct rendezvous point at the proper time. This was a huge task for VS-38 and its fleet of eight elderly Vikings.

'The coordination for these missions was immense, and due to the professionalism of the crews involved, the skills of the maintenance people back on the ship and the reliability of CVW-2's jets, we never had to divert anybody ashore. Admittedly, we were relatively low on gas as we headed out of Iraq on our way home, but the S-3s were always where they needed to be when we checked in with the carrier.

'As the war moved further north, and the larger Coalition tankers started to operate in southern Iraq, things got better for us in the Hornet as our time on station greatly increased. We could literally fill up with gas just 20 minutes' flying time from Baghdad. We would get off the tanker, check in and have tons of time to hang around on station with full tanks.'

'BLUE-ON-BLUE'

Naval TACAIR types flew an amazing 5568 combat sorties between 19 March and 18 April 2003, braving enemy AAA and SAMs, poor weather and crowded skies to ensure a Coalition victory in the shortest possible time. Thanks to rigorous pre-war training, overwhelming air superiority and sound tactics, not a single Navy aircraft was lost as a result of enemy action. However, one naval aviator *was* killed in combat in OIF, and tragically by his own side.

Lt Nathan White of CVW-5's VFA-195 had launched from CV-63 on the night of 2 April 2003 on what was supposed to be a routine KI/CAS mission in support of troops closing on Baghdad. Flying from the dedicated CAS carrier, he and his squadronmates had been heavily involved in the ground campaign from 19 March, operating with elements of V Corps in particular. White and his wingman flew into Iraq and were instructed by their E-2 controller to head for Karbala, 50 miles south of Baghdad. Elements of the 3rd Infantry Division were encountering stiff resistance in the area, and air support was requested to help clear a path for mechanised units pushing north.

It is unclear whether Lt White had already bombed his targets and was heading home or was still en route to the area when his Hornet was engaged by a US Army-manned mobile PAC-3 Patriot missile battery in south-central Iraq. His jet was destroyed by the weapon, and both the aircraft and the remains of the pilot were not found for a further ten days.

Ironically, Nathan White had briefly mentioned the threat posed by the Patriot batteries in the final e-mail message that he had sent his family before his untimely demise;

'When going in on a strike, there is always a lot going on. Here is a brief snapshot – brief for an hour or more to map out the flight, get catapulted from standstill to 140 miles an hour in less than two seconds, navigate through a maze of airborne highways that try to deconflict aircraft and of course steer you clear of the Army's Patriot batteries, jump from radio frequency to radio frequency at least 12 different times, shifting from controller to controller, avoid a sky full of AAA, surface-to-air missiles and ballistic rockets, set up your weapons system, acquire your target, drop on target, fly to an airborne tanker, join up, get gas and then fly back and land on a boat bobbing around in the middle of a sandstorm. Make it night time and throw in thunderstorms, and then it really gets exciting.'

Fellow CVW-5 Hornet pilot Lt John Allison was also attacking targets near Karbala on 2 April;

'I was airborne at the same time that Lt White was lost to the Patriot battery – I was only about ten minutes ahead of him. I had also been operating in the same area that he had been flying his CAS mission, near Karbala. This part of Iraq was always busy in OIF, with both Air Force and Navy TACAIR assets operating side-by-side. Despite being close by, I only discovered that CVW-5 had lost a jet when I got back to the ship.'

Navy pilots had been concerned about the potential threat posed by the deadly Patriot missile prior to the commencement of OIF, and these fears grew considerably after No 9 Sqn RAF lost a Tornado GR 4 that was returning to Ali Al-Salem air base, in Kuwait, from a strike mission on the morning of 23 March. VFA-151's Lt Cdr Ron Candiloro explained;

'Although I remained wary of the Iraqi SAM threat, I was actually more afraid of our own Patriot batteries. We would commonly get lit up by the missile's fire control radar, and that was really scary. These lock-ups increased in frequency as our forces moved further north into Iraq, and this prompted my CO, Cdr Hubbard, to instigate a daily briefing that told us all where the Patriot batteries were all over the country. A copy of this information was also printed onto a card that we carried with us in the

VFA-195's 'Chippy 401' (Lot XVII F/A-18C BuNo 164970) gets the signal to launch from CV-63's dual 'shooter' team on waist cat three during night ops towards the end of OIF. Although the conflict was drawing to a close when this photo was taken, CVW-5's TACAIR pilots continued to be opposed by AAA and SAMs right up until the air war ended on 18 April. VFA-192's Lt John Allison told the author;

'I found that the Iraqi AAA and SAM threat got worse as the campaign came to a close, with my missions being more opposed in the final days of OIF than they were in the beginning. This was particularly the case when attacking troops that had been bypassed north of An Nasiriyah, as well as those defending the towns east of Baghdad – I was flying kill box missions on these occasions. However, the southern areas of Iraq were pretty well AAA free by the final week of the war, whereas in the beginning you were being fired on as soon as you crossed the border. It was not until you got up to Baghdad and beyond that you got shot at, and the threat remained real in these areas until war's end.

'On my final mission in OIF, we were flying east over the suburbs of Baghdad when a SAM flashed by below us literally out of nowhere. We had not been warned of its presence by our RHAW gear because the missile had been launched unguided. When we went searching for the launch site after the missile had safely passed by, all we could see were residential streets and rows and rows of houses' (PH3 Todd Frantom)

A PAC-3 Patriot missile heads for its target during a training exercise in the USA pre-OIF. Having performed poorly in *Desert Storm* in 1991, the weapon's accuracy had been dramatically improved by the time OIF commenced. Its target identification was still lacking in certain modes, however, as Coalition TACAIR crews discovered to their cost. Unlike several of the pilots that the author interviewed, CVW-2's Capt Larry Burt seemed relatively happy with the Patriot's presence in-theatre;

'We never got any information on the losses of the Tornado and the Hornet, and we assumed that the jets did not have their Mode 4 IFF working and were coming in fast directly at the battery. We felt that the profiles we were flying were safe, and we had good indications in the cockpit if our vital Mode 4 IFF system was not responding correctly to interrogation. We checked that IFF was functioning both before and after we launched, and prior to going into Iraq. If it was faulty then we turned around and headed back to the ship. We were quite surprised when the Hornet, in particular, went down, as we did not realise that the Patriot batteries were following the Army up into Iraq. We had not been told that there were batteries as far north as Karbala. Once we knew that they were there, we were not restricted from flying over them – there was just a small three-mile circle around the operator's sight that you could not fly through, and this was for collision avoidance should he have to start firing missiles' (*DoD*)

cockpit. I felt that this was the most important briefing card issued to me before every mission, and it was always at the top of my knee war pack – I was terrified by the Patriot.

'It is by far the most lethal SAM system in the world, and there is no aeroplane in existence that is going to get away from it. The missile itself is also designed to bias its impact on the nose of the aircraft so as to kill the pilot. If a Patriot is fired at your aircraft, you might as well eject, as there is nothing you can do to get away from it.'

'We could clearly tell if a Patriot battery was looking at us, as our ALR-67 radar homing and warning system would clearly indicate that we had been locked up by the missile's search radar. When this happened, the jet's Mode 4 IFF (Identification Friend or Foe) was supposed to "squawk" (reply) to the Patriot's radar with an encrypted signal which indicated to the missile that its "target" was in fact friendly. In actuality, we of course lost two jets, which I appreciate is a small number in relation to the 40,000+ sorties that were flown, but that is no consolation to us TACAIR crews.

'The Patriot batteries were initially operated in automated mode, which meant there was no human interaction in the way it interrogated targets. For 99.9 per cent of the time, the system worked fine, but twice it did not, although there is some question as to whether the Tornado GR 4's IFF was functioning correctly when it was shot down.

'When you looked at the numbers, we all knew that there was very little chance that we would be shot down by the Patriot, but whenever I was lit up by one I started "squawking" all the modes and codes I could – and that was before we lost the Hornet off the *Kitty Hawk*. We had started to get concerned about the Patriot in automated mode after the Tornado was lost, and when the Hornet was downed we really started to question what exactly the Army was doing with the weapon. Our concerns travelled "up the chain", and that was when the Army changed the Patriot's engagement parameters from auto to manual, which meant that a human operator had to input the direction to fire. That gave us more peace of mind, but unfortunately it had cost three lives to get this change made.

'I avoided flying anywhere near a Patriot battery if I could help it, which got progressively more difficult as they were all over the place. I knew where they were all sited, however, as did most pilots in my unit.

'Psychologically, the loss of two jets to Patriot missiles had a big impact on the air wing. Heading into Iraq, I was confident that I could handle literally anything that the enemy threw at me. Indeed, I was more scared of what our guys were going to do to me, and in particular the Patriot batteries. It was a big relief when you finally got out of Iraq and left the last of the Army's missile batteries behind you near the end of every sortie.'

Lt Cdr Candiloro's boss, Cdr Hubbard, flew into Iraq soon after Lt White had been lost. He too came close to becoming a statistic that night;

'About 90 minutes after the Hornet was lost, I walked into VFA-151's ready room on the ship and was told by one of my pilots that an aircraft had been shot down right where I was heading on my next sortie. We launched and flew up there as planned, and on the way into Baghdad you could hear the various assets on the ground and in the air trying to coordinate a rescue effort in case the pilot had gotten out of his jet alive.

'Minutes after this, my wingman and I were heading north when my Hornet was rocked by a deafening explosion that temporarily blinded me. I happened to be looking out the right side of the canopy when a 105 mm round cooked off between my wingman and I – we were flying in formation, with a half-mile separation. I could not hear the radios, and the white flash had ruined my night vision. Slowly, my hearing came back, and my wingman checked in with me to see if I was alright. We quickly found our designated target – a communications site – and dropped our bombs, then headed back south as fast as we could.

'Having already had one close shave on this mission, we then almost collided with a section of F-16s heading in the opposite direction. Weather had forced us down, and we had ended up at the same height as these guys. We were so close when we passed that I could see the letters and numbers on the tail of one of the jets, as well as the reflection of the multi-function displays in the pilot's face – he was heads down, fiddling around in his cockpit. They never saw us, as we flashed past each other with a separation of just 200 ft. My wingman also saw the guy that I almost hit, and then another F-16 almost flew into him.

'This incident confirmed what I was telling my pilots in their daily briefings – "the biggest threat out here now is us". Height deconfliction was always going to be a problem, despite the various "highways" that were set up at different altitudes, as it only took some bad weather to throw these plans into disarray. And with the best will in the world, the AWACS crews cannot be expected to operate as air traffic controllers.

'I experienced a second mid-air miss several nights later while trying to attack some tanks travelling south-east of Baghdad. My FAC kept on changing the coordinates that we were supposed to attack, and I eventually told him that he had to settle down and give us the correct ones or we were not going to be able to drop our bombs.

'After six changes he finally came up with solid coordinates, and I was heads down typing these into the weapons computer when I got this weird feeling that caused me to look up and out of the cockpit. Immediately ahead of me was the dark mass of a B-1, which was so close that part of the left wing was on one side of the canopy bow and a section of the right wing was on the other side of it! I pushed the stick fully forward, and the negative G saw my helmet bag fly out from the back of the cockpit and my head smack the canopy very hard – I had loosened

VFA-151's fifteen pilots, engineering (green jersey) and ordnance (red jersey) officers pose for a squadron photograph just prior to CV-64 chopping out of the NAG in late April 2003. Squadron CO Cdr Mark Hubbard is standing fourth from left. Immediately behind his head is a low-vis rendition of the First Navy Jack, adorned with a rattlesnake and the motto *DON'T TREAD ON ME*. Cdr Hubbard explained the significance of the flag, and 'Switch 301's' *In Memory of Sandra Teague* legend;

'The Jack was first employed by Commodore Esek Hopkins in the autumn of 1775 as he readied the Continental Navy in the Delaware River. His signal for the whole fleet to engage the enemy was the striped Jack. This Jack represents a historic reminder of the Nation's and the Navy's origin, and the will to preserve and triumph. As directed by the Chief of Naval Operations in late 2001, the First Navy Jack will be flown on all US Navy ships in lieu of the Union Jack during the Global War on Terrorism to honour those who died during the attack of 11 September 2001.

'The *Sandra Teague* legend honours the memory of the fiancée of Lt(jg) Frank Huffman. Ms Teague was a passenger on American Airlines Flight 77 which crashed into the Pentagon, where Frank was working as a Navy Public Affairs Officer. He subsequently volunteered to serve as an Intelligence Collections Officer for CVW-2 aboard CV-64 during our OIF deployment' (*VFA-151*)

Navy Hornets relied heavily on FAC(A) crews flying in both Tomcats and Marine F/A-18Ds. Here, both types prepare to take on fuel en route to targets around Baghdad. The F/A-18D is from VMFA(AW)-533, which conducted its war from Al-Jaber, in Kuwait, whilst the F-14Ds are from CVW-2's VF-2. D-CAG Capt Craig Geron flew with VF-2 on a number of occasions in OIF, where he got to see just how effective the unit was at the FAC(A) mission;

'The unit had five FAC(A) crews, and these guys were kept very busy performing CAS with other Coalition assets over the battlefield. When the LGB quickly proved to be the weapon of choice for CAS due to its targeting versatility, the FAC(A) crews, and their ability to buddy-lase, really came to the fore.

'You achieved accuracy with the LGB by laser designating the target with either your own pod, your wingman's pod or by the ground FAC using a hand-held designator. The FAC(A) guys performed most of the buddy-lasing, although this was not the preferred option of attack within CVW-2. Most pilots/crews either self-lased or had the FAC on the ground designate the target' (*Capt Doug Glover*)

my lap belts earlier in the mission in order to get a little more comfortable. The impact with the canopy almost knocked me unconscious! My wingman asked me if I had seen the bomber, and I told him that I thought that it was a B-1. By then we were looking straight down its afterburner cans, which the pilot lit up as he powered away from us.

'Having missed the bomber, we confirmed with the FAC that we would be over the target in five minutes. I was carrying two JDAMs and my wingman was armed with three JSOW, and we quickly identified six tanks travelling nose to tail in the open. We confirmed with the FAC that there were no "friendlies" in the area, and then I attacked with the JDAMs on the first pass and my wingman followed up with his JSOW on the second attack run. We got good BHA on all six tanks, with one of my JDAMs registering a direct hit and the second one missing by just 50 ft.'

FAC(A)

Navy and Marine units have always been great proponents of working with forward air controllers operating from fast jet types. Known as Forward Air Controllers (Airborne), the lineage of the FAC(A) goes back to the Vietnam War, when Marine 'spotters' performed the Tactical Air Controlling (Airborne) mission in aircraft such as the TF-9J Cougar and the TA-4F Skyhawk. Today, the Marines still conduct the FAC(A) mission with their two-seat F/A-18Ds, which proved indispensable in the ground campaign of OIF.

The Navy got into the FAC(A) role a little later than the Marines, selecting the F-14 Tomcat for the mission following the aircraft's metamorphosis into a precision bomber in the mid 1990s. The only two-seat TACAIR jet operating from a carrier deck that possessed the range, speed, targeting equipment and avionics capable of performing this

highly demanding role, the jet made its FAC(A) combat debut over Kosovo in Operation *Allied Force* in March 1999. The leading role played by US naval aviation in OEF two years later saw the Tomcat FAC(A) concept prove its worth over and over again, and much was expected of the five F-14 units committed to OIF in March 2003. CVW-14's primary FAC(A) unit was VF-31, and one its regular customers was Lt Cdr Paul Olin of VFA-113;

'During the second week of the war my section was tasked with knocking out some artillery pieces northwest of Baghdad at night. We checked in with the E-2 controller, and were told to wait over Karbala for 20 minutes as a FAC(A)-crewed Tomcat from VF-31 was coming to help us get these guns after he had dealt with a more pressing target in Baghdad itself. By the time he showed up there were a number of other Air Force and Navy jets in the "queue" waiting for targets, but we got the priority because we were now running low on fuel.

'We followed the FAC(A) directly over downtown Baghdad, which was a surreal experience as it was fully lit up – I felt like I was flying over Los Angeles. For some reason there was no AAA, which was unusual as we had been opposed every other time we had flown over the city. The F-14 was below me at 10,000 ft, and we were flying at 12,000 ft, having been pushed down by the weather. I felt comfortable at this height.

'We flew several orbits while the FAC(A) crew tried to find the guns, and we had not yet got to the stage were they had started to talk our eyes onto the target when suddenly the sky erupted with AAA, interspersed with around 25 SAMs. It was at this point that we decided to abort the artillery hunt and climb to safety!'

CVW-2's Capt Larry Burt was also full of praise for the Tomcat FAC(A)s that he worked with in the latter stages of OIF, flying missions with crews from both VF-31 and VF-2;

'By early April, when we were desperately trying to acquire and prosecute targets, the Tomcat FAC(A)s really came into their own. You had lots of jets ready to drop their bombs, but there was a shortage of real targets amongst all the potential contacts that needed to be attacked. It was therefore up to the FAC(A)s to work out what were the bona fide targets by talking over the radio with the guys on the ground, liaising with airborne controllers and scouring the battlefield with their own systems. It was while performing this SCAR and FAC(A) mission that the two-man crew in the F-14 excelled. A big part of the FAC(A) mission is awareness, which comes with experience, and all of the FAC(A)-qualified crews had the latter in abundance.'

USAF and Marine jets also flew FAC(A) missions for Navy F/A-18s during OIF, as Lt Cdr Ron Candiloro related to the author;

'On one of my CAS missions, Lt Cdr Richard Thompson and I went

This abandoned SA-3 SAM battery was discovered on the outskirts of Baghdad near the end of the war by Senior MSgt Brian Aguiar and MSgt Brad Kephart of the USAF's 1st Expeditionary Air Operations Support Squadron. Literally hundreds of SAMs, and their mobile launchers, were captured intact and fully operable by Coalition troops after the Iraqi capital was seized (*USAF*)

USAF FAC(A)s also did their fair share of target spotting for Navy Hornets in OIF, with the OA/A-10A pilots proving particularly adept at this mission. This particular Thunderbolt II (78-0634) was flown by the 190th Fighter Squadron, Idaho Air National Guard, from Al-Jaber, in Kuwait. The jet is armed with two AGM-65 laser Mavericks, four Mk 82 bombs and two 2.5-in rocket pods – the contents of the latter were used primarily as target markers (*USAF*)

US Army FAC(A)s in OH-58 Kiowas also got in on the act with Navy Hornet units in OIF, particularly during the assaults on An Nasiriyah and Tikrit (*US Army*)

up to a kill box northeast of Baghdad near Tikrit. As we arrived on station, two USAF A-10 FAC(A)s were just dropping the last of their bombs on a target within the kill box. We checked in with them and they told us that it was an open kill box, with no friendlies in the area. The A-10 pilots then told us to "kill" any vehicles that we happened to spot in bunkers, talking us onto a couple of targets prior to departing.

'As we headed into the kill box, you could see the destruction that the A-10s had left in their wake – fires and plumes of smoke rose from numerous vehicles scattered in all directions below us. Lt Cdr Thompson actually thought that there was another aircraft in the area still dropping bombs because of the number of secondary explosions continuing to go off in the kill box.

'We circled around the target area, pulled out our binoculars and picked out several vehicles in bunkers that had been spared the destruction wrought by the A-10s. In what effectively became a free-for-all, we then spent the next 15 minutes rolling in and attacking targets with our JDAM and LGBs. As it turned out, this was my last sortie of OIF.'

Army and Marine attack helicopters also occasionally flew pseudo-FAC(A) missions for carrier-based Hornets, and VFA-192's Lt John Allison was one such pilot to benefit from having a helicopter both spotting and lasing for him;

'On one of the daylight urban CAS missions that I was involved in, there were soldiers on the ground that were taking fire from a four-storey building in An Nasiriyah. We duly blew the structure apart with five 500-lb LGBs that we dropped directly into it.

'We had an Army OH-58 Kiowa lasing for us on this occasion, although we also had our FLIR locked onto the building so that we knew that we were attacking the correct spot. This was the only time that I worked with a helicopter in this role. The OH-58 crew lasing the target

was talking to a FAC on the ground, who was in turn relaying targeting information to me. The FAC then told me to attack from a certain direction, giving me talk-on target instructions as to which building to aim for.

'We had to coordinate our attack with the helicopter so that our bombs were released as the OH-58 provided the laser guidance onto the building. I never saw the Kiowa at any stage in our attack, and it was only when I asked the FAC who was lasing the target that I found out

that it was a helicopter – I didn't realise they could lase targets in an OH-58 until that mission! The FAC gave us instant feedback on how accurate our bombs had been, and he was very happy with the results.

'My laser was fully functional on this mission, and I could have successfully employed it. The OH-58 was closer, however, and the pilot could see exactly what was going on. This meant that he could place the laser in exactly the right spot, whereas I might have been a little off from the height we were flying at.'

BAGHDAD INTERNATIONAL

With airpower having weakened the Republican Guard's Baghdad and Nebuchadnezzar divisions after days of continual attack, elements of V Corps' 3rd Infantry Division broke through the 'Karbala Gap' between Karbala and Lake Razzaza on 2 April. They succeeded in seizing a strategically important bridge over the Euphrates at Mussayib and now prepared for the assault on Saddam Hussein International Airport, which was just 12 miles southwest of Baghdad city centre.

On the evening of 4 April mechanised elements of the 3rd Infantry Division launched their first assault on the airport, which was defended by both Republican Guard troops of the Medina Division and Fedayeen fighters. TACAIR assets from all three NAG-based carriers found themselves heavily involved in the action which ensued, the rapidity of the American advance from Mussayib having caught the Iraqi troops off their guard. M1A2 Abrams tanks and Bradley fighting vehicles initially made good progress along the single lane road which led to the airport, but a series of near-suicidal attacks by Iraqi armoured vehicles, supported by mortar and rocket-propelled grenade fire, stalled the 3rd Infantry Division advance.

Operating from the designated day carrier in the NAG, CVW-14 was heavily involved in the opening phase of the airport assault. Indeed, aircraft from VFA-113 were amongst the first to answer the call when the Army came under attack at dusk on the 4th. The ferocity of the fighting duly resulted in several pilots from the unit being recommended for awards post-OIF, including Lt Cdr James Logsdon. The citation for his proposed (the award had not yet been confirmed when this book went to press) decoration read as follows;

'While supporting the objectives of Operation *Iraqi Freedom*, Lt Cdr Logsdon, as "Canasta 5", was the Airborne Interdiction Mission Commander of a three-ship element of F/A-18 Hornets tasked with providing aerial strike support for the first ground forces approaching Baghdad. After conducting an aerial refuelling evolution and navigating

Lt John Allison goes in search of a target in 'Dragon 306' (Lot XVII F/A-18C BuNo 164958) in early April 2003;

'The fluidity of the way we fought the war proved hugely beneficial for the troops on the ground, as I rarely knew what my target would be when I launched. We simply went where the ground forces needed us most, and on several occasions I was called up by FACs who were taking fire. My wingman and I duly took out whatever it was that was firing at them.

'On one occasion we were flying west of Baghdad, near the city's three large lakes, when we got a call from an E-2 controller telling us to attack 13 S-60 anti-aircraft guns that had been spotted in a field near one of the lakes – he cleared us to bomb anything in this field. I was leading two other Hornets, and I told one pilot to take the guns on the left, the other to take the guns on the right, and I would go for those in the middle of the field.

'We ended up taking out nine of the thirteen guns with our LGBs, and we got good secondaries from our hits. We were being fired at throughout our attacking runs, but we remained above 10,000 ft, and none of the AAA managed to reach up that high.'

Allison's jet is armed with a single GBU-12 under each wing, an AIM-9M on the starboard wingtip rail and a solitary AIM-120C (*Lt John Allison*)

Built consecutively on McDonnell Douglas' St Louis production line in the summer of 1991, 'Fist 402' (Lot XIV F/A-18C BuNo 164637) and 'Sting 301' (Lot XIV BuNo 164636) prepare to launch on an urban CAS mission on 5 April 2003. Both jets are armed with AGM-65 laser Mavericks, and they were almost certainly expended supporting British troops during the assault on Basra or covering tanks of the 3rd Infantry Division during their now-famous 'Thunder Run' into Baghdad (*US Navy*)

US Army FACs call in air strikes during the 3rd Infantry Division's assault on Saddam Hussein International Airport on the evening of 4 April 2003 (*US Army*)

over 400 miles, Lt Cdr Logsdon received urgent tasking to immediately contact "Advance 51", the US Army 3rd Infantry Division FAC embedded in an armoured column advancing east on Highway 10, northwest of Baghdad Airport. "Advance 51" communicated that his armoured column had advanced into an ambush and was under heavy and intense fire. "Advance 51" also transmitted in distress that they were quickly falling back and needed bombs to suppress the enemy onslaught. The radio calls from "Advance 51" were sometimes drowned out by the sounds of the Armoured Personnel Carrier's engine racing during their retreat.

'With all electronic targeting aides unusable due to low light levels, Lt Cdr Logsdon was forced to descend below the minimum safe altitude to ensure he had targeted the correct troops and tanks. His weapon release forced him to bottom out over Baghdad International Airport at 6000 ft – the heart of the AAA envelope. From this initial bomb impact, the FAC was able to direct his eyes to additional troops and armour hidden in the tree lines.

'Undeterred by heavy AAA being fired at his aircraft, and warnings from "Advance 51" that ZSU-23 "Gundish" units had been spotted in the area, he immediately manoeuvred his jet for multiple attacks on the troops and armoured vehicles leading the ambush on the American forces. In the face of danger, he remained engaged for multiple runs at low altitude to deliver weapons, spot more targets, and then provide cover for his wingmen's deliveries, with repeated exposure to concentrated enemy fire. After destroying six separate targets (troops, tanks and armoured vehicles), Lt Cdr Logsdon's flight had stopped the Iraqi attack on the retreating US Army column. The FAC confirmed the extraordinary troop support and the effectiveness of Lt Cdr Logsdon's devastating attacks.

'His actions allowed for the immediate suppression of the Medina Republican Guard ambush without injuries to friendly forces. Additionally, his selfless and heroic actions saved American lives, while risking his own repeatedly.'

Capt Larry Burt was still flying with CVW-14 at the time of the airport assault, and his first mission on the evening of 4 April provided him with some of his most vivid memories of OIF;

'My weirdest mission took place while hitting targets around Baghdad International Airport on the day ground forces actually attacked it for the first time. We were flying at dusk, so there was still enough light for us to be highlighted in the sky, and we were getting a lot of AAA fired at us. When you looked down at the airport you could see all these muzzle flashes and jets rolling in and dropping bombs, yet running right alongside the airport was a four-lane highway, and it was rush hour! It was the most surreal thing I had ever seen. There was Baghdad on the verge of invasion, and most of the population were going about their daily business.

'Our FAC was in very close contact with the enemy on this mission, being just a few thousand feet away from where our bombs were detonating. He was talking to us in spurts, having to take cover as his position came under fire. He would shout, "Stand by", and then you would hear nothing for 60 seconds. He would come back on the radio and tell us "we are taking mortar fire". Unfazed, the FAC would then talk us onto the target. I could see some HUMVEEs and tanks spread out opposite a canal, and the FAC told us that he thought that the mortar rounds were coming from the far side of the waterway. I replied, "Okay, I've got it", and duly dropped LGBs on the area. We must have hit the mortar team, as the FAC quickly told us that the shelling had stopped.'

CVW-2 was also called in to lend support as the battle for Saddam International raged across the southern perimeter of the airport. CAG staffer Lt Cdr Zeno Rausa was called into action as darkness enveloped the area on 4 April;

'We were directed to take out an artillery piece that was shooting at our boys on the deck. You would think any thing around an airport would be easy to find. Well it took several passes that brought me down to the "mid teens" to find this thing on my FLIR sensor. All the while, there was AAA firing to my west and east – an entire battery of AAA appeared to be firing away several miles to the east of me, and there was a Coalition aircraft working on a different frequency that was down a lot lower than me. He was weaving, and the tracers surrounded his aircraft. The same was happening to another Coalition aircraft who was also low, dodging AAA of a bigger calibre somewhere near Al Taqaddum, to the west of Baghdad. I thought to myself that these guys must be on drugs, or be helping some of our guys on the deck who were in serious trouble, to fly that low. I felt pretty comfortable at my altitude, considering what I was watching.

'I had a "nugget" with me, and he was struggling to pick up the target himself. We were getting a talk-on second hand, Army scouts on the deck passing the target coordinates and a target area description to a ground FAC, who then passed them to us. As I became more familiar with the target area, and finally picked up the artillery piece, I told the scouts to stay clear of it. The

'Fist 410' (Lot XIV F/A-18C BuNo 164676) returns to CVN-72 on 5 April 2003 with its laser Mavericks still on attached to their pylons. Target opportunities rapidly diminished following the capture of Baghdad's international airport. VFA-25's Cdr Don Braswell had some interesting views on the way TACAIR assets were used in OIF, which he shared with the author;

'There has been a lot of talk about CAS in OIF, and I think this may be one of the misconceptions coming out of the way we fought the war. A couple of times I spoke with guys on the ground who were within one or two miles of the target, and more CAS missions cropped up as ground forces closed on Baghdad. However, for much of the war my squadron flew a lot of SCAR sorties, where a controller would give you a waypoint that was close to a military target. From 20,000 ft, you are not going to see a muzzle flash seven miles away, so you had to rely on the guys on the ground to give you accurate coordinates. When flying a typical OIF SCAR sortie, it was unlikely that you would be able to PID the target as you would have done in a "classical" CAS mission.

'As much as my aviation bubbas might not like to hear this, as with OEF, OIF was an Army, Marine Corps, Special Operations war, and we were there, as we almost always are, simply in assist mode. They can do a lot of stuff with artillery and helicopters. We can bring a bigger punch if required, although not as often. They use us where they want us' (*US Navy*)

gun's crew wasn't firing any more, having almost certainly heard us circling overhead. The barrel of the weapon was still hot, however, making it easily identifiable via FLIR once you were looking in the right area.

'I dived at the target and guided a GBU-12 onto the weapon, seeing "metal-on-metal". Pieces flew off the gun into the dust, but there was no explosion – my bomb was a dud. I then talked my wingman onto the target to finish it off. He "shacked" the gun, and his bomb went high order. GBUs are so damn accurate.'

VFA-137 CO Cdr Walt Stammer helped the Army seize the airport on the evening of 5 April after 24 hours of literally hand-to-hand combat across the site;

'I was airborne when the Army captured Saddam International Airport, and we did some good work over the target hitting AAA sites and mortar pits, as well as some ammunition storage bunkers – I had a massive secondary explosion from one of those, which I hit with an LGB. I could see a number of civilian airliners parked on the various taxiways and ramps, and we were told by our E-2 controller not to attack them. However, when the Army guys advanced on the airport they destroyed a number of these aircraft. I could see all of this unfolding before me through my NVGs as I circled at altitude over the area.

'I was very familiar with the airport's layout, as I had led a strike that had levelled out all the Republican Guard barracks and the watch towers on the south-east side of the runways on night three of OIF. Thanks to this mission, the Army met far less resistance than it had expected when it attacked Saddam International.'

END GAME

Within a day of the airport being seized, the first tanks of the 3rd Infantry Division had entered southern Baghdad as part of the audacious Operation *Thunder Run*. By 9 April Marines of the 1st MEF had occupied Firdaus Square in central Baghdad, where they helped local residents topple a 20 ft statue of Saddam Hussein under the gaze of the world's media. Although for many observers this signalled the end of the struggle to capture Baghdad, fighting continued across Iraq. As if to prove this point, the following day Coalition strike aircraft flew 550 sorties, the bulk of which were against Iraqi positions in and around Baghdad. One such mission was flown by CVW-2's Capt Mark Fox;

'I was flying the night that the 3rd Infantry Division advanced into Baghdad, and there were firefights all over the city. We checked in with a FAC and he talked us onto the target. He told me that there was a big race track near Baghdad International Airport, and that the enemy was holed up in a clutch of APCs parked in a nearby treeline. His target description was so good that

SSgt Brandon Storey secures a road next to a destroyed Iraqi APC during a patrol of the Baghdad suburbs. Storey served as a FAC with the 1st Expeditionary Air Operations Support Squadron during OIF, guiding Navy as well as Air Force TACAIR types in combat (*USAF*)

even the NITE Hawk could pick up the target. I was lasing the APCs with my pod, and literally about ten seconds away from pickling an LGB, when the FAC shouted, "ABORT, ABORT, ABORT. We've got friendlies sweeping through there".

'The synergy between what was going on on the ground and what was going on in the air was amazing that night, as this close call proved. The frontline was at its most fluid during the final push into Baghdad.

'Flying over the city that night at 20,000 ft was a most interesting experience, for all the guys who had previously been paid to shoot up at us were distracted by the 3rd Infantry Division, leaving the skies virtually free of AAA.'

Having been in the NAG since mid-December 2002, and having led the first 'Shock and Awe' strike on Baghdad on 21 March, Capt Fox flew his 14th, and last, OIF mission on 15 April 2003. With his time as Commander of CVW-2 having been extended from January to mid-April, CAG Fox was duly relieved by his deputy, Capt Craig Geron.

Capt Mark Fox receives a traditional welcome back aboard CV-64 from CAG 'Paddles', Lt Cdr 'Steamer' Raupp, after completing his final OIF flight as commander of CVW-2 on 15 April 2003. Fox flew 14 combat missions during the war, returning to the carrier with his ordnance still on the wing pylons on the last three of these sorties due to a lack tasking. The CVW-2 Change of Command ceremony took place on 16 April, and within a week of his last OIF sortie, Capt Fox was in the White House interviewing for his current job as Deputy Director of the White House Military Office – out of one interesting tour into another! In April 2004, Capt Fox was awarded one of only a handful of Distinguished Flying Crosses bestowed on naval aviators post-OIF. Presented to him by President George W Bush, Capt Fox received this award for leading the first OIF strike on Baghdad. (*US Navy*)

NIMITZ IN, *LINCOLN* OUT

By the time Baghdad fell, the *Lincoln* battle group had at last been relieved in the NAG by USS *Nimitz* (CVN-68), with CVW-11 embarked – the switch over took place in the NAG on 7 April. Having been on deployment for nine months, CVN-72 headed home at the end of the longest cruise for a US carrier since 1973. As the day carrier in the NAG, *Lincoln* had played a major part in OIF, CVW-14 dropping more than 1.3 million pounds of ordnance in the first 17 days of the conflict.

CVN-68 duly took up the role of the day carrier, the *Nimitz* seeing combat within hours of arriving in the NAG as Commander of CVW-11, Capt Chuck Wright, explained;

'We had sailed through the Strait of Hormuz on 6 April, and had scheduled a day of regular ops for the 7th in order to familiarise ourselves with flying in the Gulf. That evening we were performing night traps when we got the call over the SIPRNET to send an E-2 over the beach as a replacement for an aircraft that had gone unserviceable. This proved to be a seamless introduction to combat ops for CVW-11, as we had got onto the SIPRNET "shotgun" as soon as we deployed on 3 March in order to keep tabs on all the ATO notes from the CAOC at "PSAB". We therefore had more information than we could digest on how the war was being waged from a naval aviation point of view. This allowed us to keep a close watch on the development of the ATO in-theatre.

'As we approached the strait, we began to run our own mirror-image of the "driveways" in OIF. The administrative side of flying combat missions was the "cruncher" for "Joe aviator" in this war, and we wanted to make sure that our guys were well prepared before they arrived in-theatre. They needed to know who to check in with after taking off, how not to get violated by straying into the wrong airspace, how not to piss off every other agency operating in OIF, how not to have a mid-air collision and how to get to the target and back. We duly recreated these airspace procedures for the air wing over the Indian Ocean, using our E-2s to simulate all the controlling agencies we would encounter in the Gulf. This in turn allowed our Hawkeyes to work straight into the OIF campaign a day earlier than we expected, and the rest of CVW-11 took up where CVW-14 left off on 8 April.

'Our Hornet units got to drop bombs from the first day we arrived on station, and the bulk of the missions that we flew were KI/CAS, although we did perform a handful of designated strikes. The latter were flown by sections of Super Hornets flying up around Mosul and Tikrit, which attacked barracks with JDAM. These strikes totalled just four to eight sorties out of the 60 to 80 that we were flying per day at that stage of the war.'

Targets became progressively more scarce following the capture of Baghdad, and Hornet pilots were now regularly returning to their ships with their bombs still on the pylons. VFA-151's Lt Cdr Ron Candiloro was one of those naval aviators who struggled to get his bombs off in the final ten days of OIF;

'By the middle of the war the targets began to get more scarce, and this was a direct result of the amount of ordnance we had dropped. From the second OIF started to the end of the war three weeks later, there was a bomb blowing up in Iraq literally every 15 seconds. Flying from the night carrier, the bulk of my missions took place in the hours of darkness, and on the horizon wherever you looked you would see a bomb going off.

'As the target list began to dwindle, you would often fly into Iraq without an assigned target to hit. We would check in with the E-2 controller and they would not have a target for us to attack, or if they did, we would be in a queue behind six other guys! Often, by the time we got to the front of the queue we would be either out of "gas" or out of time, and we would have to come back to the ship – I brought my bombs back on 50 per cent of my combat sorties. We usually sortied with recoverable loads, although we went with maximum ordnance, non-recoverable load-outs in the first few missions of the war.

'All OIF carriers operated on a very rigid timescale, and had set cycle launch and recovery times. Unlike a runway ashore, which is usually open 24 hours a day, you cannot mess with the carrier's flight schedule. Having said that, the golden rule for us at all times was if anyone on the ground

The pilot of VFA-94's 'Hobo 400' (BuNo 164048) selects afterburner and prepares to launch from CVN-68's waist cat three in the last days of OIF. Arriving on station in the NAG on 8 April 2003, *Nimitz* replaced *Lincoln* as the designated day carrier. VFA-94 initially flew 14 to 16 CAS missions per day over Iraq, although by 18 April this number had dropped to six. VFA-94 flew some 500 combat missions in support of Coalition forces in Iraq both during and after OIF (*VFA-94*)

was in danger you blew off all the rules to help them. You figured out a reasonable fuel bingo level that still allowed you to get to the nearest divert field, and you did whatever was necessary to help the guys on the ground.'

The final bombs dropped by carrier-based TACAIR assets in OIF were expended on 17 April by Hornets flying from CVW-11. Although arriving in-theatre after much of the heavy fighting had ended, the four Hornet units aboard CVN-68 still made a significant contribution to

the Coalition victory in the final ten days of the conflict, as well as in the aftermath when *Nimitz* became the sole carrier in the NAG. Capt Chuck Wright recalled;

'We dropped our last bomb in OIF on 17 April, after which things went quiet for us in terms of attacking Iraqi targets. Running from noon to midnight, we generated between 65 and 75 sorties over the beach per day during the war, which we could have sustained indefinitely. By the time the conflict ended, VFA-14, -41 and -94 had dropped around 70,000 lbs of ordnance – VFA-97 did not drop any bombs. We fired some laser Mavericks, some GBU-12s, a few 1000-lb JDAM and quite a few 2000-lb JDAM. VFA-14 performed all the long-range missions to the north, where it expended a considerable number of JDAM, while VFA-41 carried out the FAC(A) work with a non-FAC(A) wingman. The latter unit shot off the bulk of the laser Mavericks while flying these missions, with VFA-94 also expending some as well.

'Post-17 April, we started to perform CAS training missions with Army FACs on the ground in order to keep our skill levels honed. We flew simulated talk-on CAS sorties against abandoned military compounds all over Iraq, and that way if someone accidentally dropped a bomb – these flights were always flown with live ordnance – it would not inflict any casualties. Such missions were comparatively rare, however, and most of the time you were just flying around on call, talking to one of the three Air Support Operations Centers (ASOCs) that now control Iraqi airspace – we usually worked with the ASOC in Baghdad.'

With its ordnance unexpended, 'Fist 411' (Lot XIV F/A-18C 164645) looks good for a two-wire recovery on CVN-72 at the end of the carrier's marathon spell on the line in the NAG. Aside from its near-mandatory AAS-38B NITE Hawk pod, affixed to the port fuselage pylon, this aircraft also boasts an ASQ-173 Laser Spot Tracker (LST) on the starboard fuselage pylon in place of an AIM-120C. The LST locates and tracks the laser light reflected off a target being designated by a second aircraft or by a ground-based laser. It can only be used to guide LGBs in daylight. VFA-25 expended 11 GBU-31s, 64 GBU-35s, 171 GBU-12s, two GBU-16s, 24 JSOW and 20 'others' ('slick' bombs and laser Mavericks) during OIF (*US Navy*)

Taking up where VFA-115's Super Hornets had left off, the F/A-18Es of CVW-11's VFA-14 were gainfully employed as tactical tankers during CVN-68's spell in the NAG. The unit also dropped JDAM in northern Iraq in the final days of the war (*VFA-94*)

When CVN-65 relieved CVN-68 in the NAG in October 2003, the TACAIR mission passed to CVW-1. One of the units to experience combat with the air wing over Iraq was VFA-82, whose CAG jet (Lot XX F/A-18C BuNo 165200) is seen here on 14 November 2003 (*US Navy*)

CVN-73 and CVW-7 commenced its spell in the NAG on 1 March 2004 (*US Navy*)

OPERATION *DESERT SCORPION*

The *Constellation* battle group departed the NAG on 17 April, leaving *Nimitz's* air wing to conduct Operation *Desert Scorpion*, which replaced OIF. Although rarely dropping any ordnance during their remaining time in-theatre, the Hornet units performed innumerable reconnaissance missions over the country, as well as exercising with local air forces in the region. CVW-11 also provided simultaneous power projection for both the Fifth and Seventh Fleets over a five-week period in an area of responsibility extending from Iraq and the NAG to North Korea. Anti-terrorist patrols were also flown off the Somalian coast. Finally, Hornets from CVN-68 escorted President George W Bush and 'Air Force One' when he visited Qatar in early June 2003.

Relieved on station in the NAG by USS *Enterprise* (CVN-65) and CVW-1 in October 2003, CVN-68 became the last OIF carrier to arrive home when it returned to the USA on 5 November following an eight-month deployment.

With Iraq rocked by a wave of suicide bombings, and increased attacks on Coalition forces by Fedayeen fighters, CVW-1 was called into action on 28 November 2003 when two Marine Corps F/A-18A+s from VMFA-312 attacked a mortar pit in eastern Baghdad with JDAM. A second bombing mission was undertaken by two F/A-18Cs from VFA-86 on 9 January 2004, each of which dropped a single 1000-lb JDAM on a mortar position near the town of Balad, north of Baghdad.

As these words are written exactly one year after OIF commenced, CVW-7's two Hornet units are conducting operations with the Fifth Fleet in the NAG from the flight deck of the USS *George Washington* (CVN-73). Saddam Hussein has been captured and his regime removed from power, yet US Navy Hornets still remain a regular sight in the skies over Iraq.

SUPER HORNETS IN OIF

Having made its combat debut in the final months of OSW, the Super Hornet went on to play a crucial role in OIF both as a strike bomber and a tactical tanker. VFA-115 was in the vanguard of 'Shock and Awe', participating in all of CVW-14's opening strikes against a series of fixed targets across southern Iraq. One of those missions was led by XO Cdr Dale Horan on the night of 22 March 2003;

'On the second night of the war I planned and led a high altitude JDAM strike on targets in Baghdad. The overall strike package consisted of around 25 aircraft, some of which were Air Force types. My division consisted of my wingman and I and a Tomcat, and immediately ahead of us were two more Hornets.

'As we got to Baghdad, we were greeted by some 30+ SAMs coming up at us, which quickly got my attention! These all seemed to be aimed at our fairly small formation of five jets. The radio burst into life with calls from the Tomcat's RIO, who did a great job spotting the missiles. "Watch out, here come two more. Hey they're guiding on you – look out. They're coming after you'. Whether they were guided or not was irrelevant to me at the time, as I was twisting and turning, performing all my best defensive manoeuvres, while simultaneously pumping out as many expendables as I could – I was not trying to save "Uncle Sam" money that night by being miserly in my use of chaff and flares.

'The good thing was that these SAMs did not prevent us from putting our bombs on the target, despite having to deviate from our course in

'Talon 203' (Lot XXIII F/A-18E BuNo 165783) and 'Talon 210' (Lot XXIII F/A-18E BuNo 165789) sit idling on the deck of CVN-72 prior to being unchained and marshalled to the catapults on 22 March 2003. Both jets feature nose art, and 'Talon 210' also boasts two JDAM silhouettes below the cockpit following bomb drops in OSW. VFA-115 CO Cdr Jeff Penfield saw action on the night that this photograph was taken;

'We were sent to bomb artillery pieces on the northern and western outskirts of Baghdad. There were three jets in my division, and we had to spend a lot of time in the SuperMEZ during the course of the mission. That night I saw more SAMs and AAA than on any other night in OIF. Falling back on our training, we saw the threat, called all the missiles and manoeuvred accordingly. We all got our LGBs off as required – despite the opposition – having found our targets, locked them up with the FLIR and then guided our bombs home' (*VFA-115*)

order to defeat the missile threat. We kept our speed up throughout the defensive manoeuvres and made sure we got back on course as quickly as we could. This meant that we still arrived over the target area on time, and it was then just a simple matter of dropping our JDAM in the GPS "basket".'

VFA-115's CO, Cdr Jeffrey Penfield, also had a close shave with a SAM during OIF;

'You never got comfortable or complacent about SAMs and AAA, but after a while you did get used to it being there on every mission, particularly those over Baghdad. One night well into the war, there were five of us – two Tomcats and three Super Hornets – heading for a target, all armed with JDAM, and my wingman spotted a SAM coming up from the left side of the formation. I then picked it up and led the formation away to the right.

'Most of the stuff up until then had been fired unguided, and we expected to see the missile fall away behind us as we manoeuvred. I thought I saw it do just that, so I turned my attention back towards the target and called for the formation to resume its previous heading. At that moment the same wingman who had initially spotted the SAM got on the radio again and said, "Skipper, it's guiding"! I immediately called for a hard left turn and we all pulled around inside the missile. As it flew down beneath my aeroplane, we reversed the direction of our turn. Just as we were reversing, the weapon exploded, lighting up both the high overcast above us and our cockpits. This all looked pretty impressive through our NVGs. We weren't fazed though, and my division went on and dropped 18 JDAM on the target just minutes later.'

After four days of attacking fixed targets, CVW-14 switched to the KI/CAS and BAI mission, and it was while serving as tactical tankers in support of TACAIR assets embroiled in the land war that VFA-115 really proved the worth of the Super Hornet in OIF, as Cdr Penfield explained;

Although boasting a greater range on internal fuel than the 'legacy' Hornet, the F/A-18Es of VFA-115 still used 'big wing' tankers in 'Shock and Awe' (VFA-115)

From day one of OIF, VFA-115 exploited the F/A-18E's ability to deliver four 2000-lb GBU-31(V)2/B JDAM during the course of a single mission. Only the F-14B/D could replicate such a load out, as the 'legacy' Hornet was restricted by range considerations. Hooked up to bow cat one, 'Talon 214' (BuNo 165792) carries just such a load. JDAM and the Super Hornet forged an unbeatable partnership, as VFA-115's Cdr Dale Horan recalled;

'I dropped four JDAMs on four separate targets spread over some 200 miles. I had launched with my wingman without knowing my targets, and I got the coordinates for my fourth target from a FAC as I was en route to bomb the third one (VFA-115)

'When we shifted from strategic attack to KI/CAS, the "big wing" tanking became limited. They were prioritised for the guys doing the strategic attack missions, and there just wasn't enough "gas" airborne for those of us going across the beach for CAS. That was not good, because protecting the troops on the ground is always priority number one for any fighter pilot. We knew that this was an important mission, but we were struggling to work out a way of continuing CAS without tanker support.

'We eventually devised a scheme whereby four of my twelve E-models would be configured in the "five-wet" tanker fit, and these jets would be flown over and over again every day. A section of strikers would join up with a single Super Hornet tanker, and they would be topped off soon after launching and then dragged into Iraq, before being topped off again around 100 miles short of the target area. The strikers could be F-14s, C-model Hornets or F/A-18Es. Having given fuel for a second time, the tanker would turn around and go home, leaving the strikers to do their work. When they came out they would get "gas" from an S-3 on their way back to the ship. Our jets were performing the tanking mission some 18 to 20 times a day, and during the course of the campaign we put 434 sorties across the beach and well into Iraq that CVW-14 could not have done without the "five-wet" Super Hornet.

'We would typically launch two tankers per cycle, and they would split up and service a pair of strikers. The "five-wet" Super Hornet would be operating on an hour-and-a-half cycle, and thanks to the fuel that the jet had transferred prior to its return to the ship, the strikers would be on a three-hour cycle. The tanker would land, refuel and then be launched again on the next cycle. VFA-115 was flying 30+ sorties a day operating on this basis, and about half of this number were tanker missions – by war's end most of my pilots had an even split between tanker sorties and strike missions. The remaining TACAIR units in CVW-14 averaged 20+ sorties per day by comparison.

'We would go about as far as we could with the tanker in about 45 minutes, as the jet had to be back on the deck within a 90-minute cycle in order for its tanks to be replenished so that it could be used again to support another section of strikers. Carrier decks don't stay open forever, so we had to be back according to our briefed recovery time.

'You max out the aeroplane when you put all that gas into it. We were launching in full afterburner at an all up weight of 66,000 lbs – around half of which was fuel – during the "five-wet" missions. The Super Hornet carries this extra weight a lot better than the F/A-18C, however, thanks to its bigger wing and more powerful engines. Nevertheless, you can feel that the jet is laden down when flying in this configuration. We were also top-end speed limited on cruise due to NAVAIR having not yet fully tested the "five-wet" aeroplane. Indeed, when we left home on 20 July 2002, NAVAIR were still not sure whether the "five-wet" tanker was going to be cleared

VFA-115's CAG jet (BuNo 165781) was one of four F/A-18Es configured as tankers within days of OIF commencing. These jets were flown literally round the clock at high all-up weights, yet the burden of extra missions had no effect on the serviceability of the jets. This had been an area of some concern for Cdr Jeff Penfield prior to the deployment;

'The biggest unknown for me about the Super Hornet pre-cruise was its durability during sustained deck ops. I had no doubts about it from an operational standpoint, but the longest we had had the jets on the boat for any one time prior to deploying was a month. Aside from the aircraft's reliability, I was also concerned about how the whole logistics support infrastructure for the Super Hornet was going to work.

'In both cases, by the end of the marathon ten-month cruise, where you expected the numbers to be the highest, we were the highest, and where you expected the numbers to be the lowest, we were the lowest. We had the highest sortie rate and the lowest maintenance hours per flying hour – eight to nine. The latter figure was achievable because the F/A-18E is easy to work on and the logistic trail was mature enough whereby we had the parts on hand to get the aeroplanes up and flying' (VFA-115)

Lt John Turner walks out to his F/A-18E on 27 March 2003 at the start of yet another CAS mission, his jet armed with 1000-lb GBU-16 LGBs and AIM-120C AMRAAM. Not yet cleared by NAVAIR to drop the ubiquitous GBU-12 LGB (CVW-11's Super Hornet units were given approval to use the weapon on 10 April 2003) or GBU-35 JDAM by the time OIF commenced, VFA-115 instead employed the larger GBU-16 LGB and GBU-31 JDAM. The unit dropped 105 GBU-31s, 70 GBU-16s, three JSOW and 30 'others' ('slick' bombs and laser Mavericks) during OIF (*US Navy*)

The pilot of 'Talon 211' (BuNo 165790) keeps an eye on the red-shirted squadron 'ordies' as they carry out some last-minute work on the guidance fins of his GBU-16. His jet is sat over waist cat four, although it has not yet been brought forward for connection to the launch shuttle. The F/A-18E is carrying four Mk 82 'slicks', split between two BRU-33 Canted Vertical Ejector Racks, beneath its starboard wing (*VFA-115*)

BuNo 165781 breaks away from the camera to reveal its warload of two 2000-lb GBU-31(V)2/B JDAM. The outward angling of the six underwing pylons is clearly visible in this photograph. One of the main selling points of the Super Hornet is its bigger wing and two extra external stores stations, which have been angled out (the six inner pylons by four degrees and the two outer pylons by 3.5 degrees) to ensure safe weapons separation (*VFA-115*)

for this deployment or not. They basically asked us what speed we felt was high enough with the jet in this configuration and we gave them a number, and my pilots were at that number during OIF. The aircraft could easily exceed this, but the test had not yet been done by the time OIF kicked off.'

Like most pilots in VFA-115, Lt John Turner got to fly his fair share of tactical tanker missions in OIF;

'The names of the tanker pilots were amongst the first written into the flight schedule every single day for the last two weeks of CVW-14's

'Talon 202' (BuNo 165783) has a GBU-16 loaded onto station three on 3 April 2003. VFA-115's ordnance team are using a fuel-powered Single Hoist Ordnance Loading System to lift the 2000-lb bomb from its Aero-12C skid up to the SUU-79/A pylon (*US Navy*)

commitment to OIF. A pilot got his tanker qualifications by conducting in-house training flights both before and during our deployment. We did not allow brand new pilots on the squadron to fly the tankers because when a jet is plugged in and refuelling, the Super Hornet pilot assumes the role of section leader. By the time we got into OIF, only two of the sixteen pilots in VFA-115 had not achieved their section leader qualification, so these new guys were the only ones not to fly tanker missions.

'Learning to fly the jet in tanker configuration is hardly rocket science, and it is not taught at the training squadron at Lemoore. To perform this mission, the pilot really only needs to know what the jet's limitations are when in the "five-wet" fit, and how to operate the buddy store. Every Super Hornet pilot would, of course, have rather been flying the jet tactically instead of as a tanker, but the mindset of VFA-115 was that we would employ these aircraft in the way that best suited CVW-14's needs in its prosecution of the war.

'The pods we used on the tanker were similar to those employed by the S-3s, although ours were a little more "beefed up" in order to cope with the high-gs and greater speeds associated with the Super Hornet. We could also use a standard buddy store taken straight off a Viking if we had to, although we preferred to fly with the strengthened version so that we could operate at a tactical speed, rather than at the S-3's speed.'

F/A-18E BuNo 165871 was one of two Super Hornets forward-deployed to CVN-72 by CVN-68-based VFA-14 on 30 March 2003. These jets were used exclusively as tankers during their week-long stay on the *Lincoln*, being flown two to three times per day in support of CVW-14's TACAIR assets (*US Navy*)

VFA-41 AT WAR

VFA-115 was not the only Super Hornet unit to see action in OIF, as in late March the squadron was boosted by the arrival of two F/A-18Es and two F/A-18Fs from CVW-11's VFA-14 and VFA-41, respectively. Four pilots and two Weapons System Operators (WSOs) were chosen to forward-deploy these jets to CVN-72 in the NAG, and one of the naval aviators

Lt Cdrs Mark Weisgerber (right) and Brian Garrison (left) deplane following their arrival aboard CVN-72 at the end of a marathon 2700-mile, 6.8-hour flight from Diego Garcia on 31 March 2003. Just 12 hours later the crew were briefing for their first mission in OIF (*Lt Cdr Mark Weisgerber*)

selected was VFA-41's Lt Cdr Mark Weisgerber. He kept a detailed diary of his time on the *Lincoln*;

'In late March, a request for more organic tanking capability and more FAC(A) crews was made by CTF-50. CVW-11 responded by putting together a plan to send two F/A-18Fs (with FAC(A)-qualified aircrew) and two F/A-18Es to CVN-72. Each aircraft was configured with four 480-gallon drop tanks and an Airborne Refueling Store (ARS).

'When the four-aeroplane detachment launched from the *Nimitz* on 30 March, we were approximately 1600 miles from the island of Diego Garcia – our overnight destination for refuelling and meeting a USAF KC-135R. The effort to get to here involved an elaborate and well executed organic tanker plan involving three S-3Bs, two F/A-18Es and an F/A-18F, which kept our four jets topped up until we were about 400 miles from the carrier. They then turned back and left us to press on to Diego Garcia alone.

'After the five-hour journey to Diego Garcia, all four aircraft were refuelled and the aircrew prepared for the 2700-mile/6.8-hour final leg to the *Lincoln*. We were escorted about half of the way by the KC-135R that had sortied from Diego Garcia, the tanker then rendevousing with another KC-135 that took us into the southern Arabian Gulf. From there, we were on our own for the final hour of flight time to the *Lincoln*.

'Upon landing on the carrier, it was immediately evident to us that this vessel was in the middle of heavy combat ops – the flight deck was crowded, but not with aircraft, since at least 50 per cent of *Lincoln's* deckload was airborne at any one time. It was crowded with various precision ordnance – GBU-12s and -16s, JDAM and JSOW, as well as AIM-120 AMRAAM and AIM-9M Sidewinders. We were all thoroughly impressed by the intensity and enthusiasm of the junior enlisted on the flight deck. It was pure professionalism from the directors to the plane captains to the ordnancemen, all working in harmony.

'Our arrival on *Lincoln* was covered by a media blitz for reasons unknown to us. After dealing with the press, we were reunited with many fellow aviators assigned to VFA-115 – all friends that I had flown with or instructed while assigned to the Super Hornet Fleet Replacement Squadron, VFA-122. Within 12 hours of completing our 4000-mile journey, the FAC(A) aircrew from VFA-41 were briefing for combat.

'Flight briefing was efficient. A typical briefing flow involved meeting 2.5 hrs prior to launch in the CV Intelligence Center, where we were provided with all the information required to execute our planned tactics – SAM updates and recent activity, positions of friendlies, position and composition of enemy troops, changes to the Air Tasking Order, etc.

'Our aircraft had been quickly re-configured soon after we arrived on CVN-72, the ARS "buddy stores" on the two VFA-41 jets being utilised by VFA-115 and our extra drop tanks being set aside as spares. During our time on *Lincoln*, both F/A-18Fs typically carried two drop tanks, two GBU-16s (1000-lb LGBs) or two JDAM, two AIM-9Ms, one AIM-120C and a full belt of 350 20 mm cannon shells.

'Our first flight in OIF took the form of a strike familiarisation sortie, where we saw first hand the myriad of controlling agencies and tanker tracks that were essential in support of our mission. My wingman was Lt John Turner from VFA-115, who expertly showed us the ropes – the end result was two destroyed BMPs, which were found just west of Baghdad International Airport in revetments.

'After our break-in hop, we spent the next five days executing our primary tasking as FAC(A)s in support of V Corps and, occasionally, the 1st MEF. We typically flew six-hour missions as a flight of two, paired up with an F-14D from VF-31. We flew with CVW-14's Tomcats primarily, because they too were FAC(A)-crewed in the main, and we initially worked as their wingmen while they "showed us the ropes". We were taking missions fragged for them on the ATO, as this was the most expeditious way to get the F/A-18Fs working effectively in-theatre. CVW-14 tried to front load both VFA-41 crews so that we could get as much combat experience as possible in a short space of time, and then take this to *Nimitz*, which was scheduled to relieve *Lincoln*.

'Our missions had a predictable flow – launch off the ship, proceed to a USAF tanker, head into country for our first Vul window (about one hour), back to the tanker, back for our second Vul window (also about one hour), back to the tanker and then back for the night trap onboard *Lincoln*. Obviously, the Vul windows were where most of the excitement took place – although joining on a tanker at night in bad weather can be exciting as well.

'On 2 April my WSO, Lt Cdr Brian Garrison, and I conducted a night mission near Karbala, worked with an Army ground unit to target some weapons bunkers just north of friendly lines. Typically, the ground forces would provide us with geographic coordinates and then attempt to talk us onto the target area using 1:50,000 charts and imagery. We would ingress the target area, attempt to locate a common reference point and then use our ASQ-228 Advanced Targeting Forward Looking Infra-Red (ATFLIR) targeting pod and NVGs to locate the actual target.

'This mission gave us our first experience with AAA, as we saw sporadic muzzle flashes on the ground (very distinctive on NVGs) followed by airbursts seconds later. Thankfully, most of the latter were not at our altitude due to the enemy's radar capability having been severely degraded by this time. After some reconnaissance of the area, we located our targets and dropped a single LGB apiece, destroying two bunkers. Following our mid-cycle tanking, we flowed north back into country and were assigned a new sector east of our previous position, and a little closer to Baghdad.

'As we approached the city, the volume of fire definitely increased. Thankfully it was mostly unguided, and not necessarily aimed at us – NVGs have a tendency to make everything appear closer than it is. Arriving at our new sector, we had a burst of AAA explode co-altitude between our two aircraft (we were about one mile apart) – the closest

Having just been unchained, VFA-14's F/A-18E BuNo 165863 is directed aft towards the waist catapults at the start of yet another OIF launch cycle aboard CVN-72 on 4 April 2003. Although the Super Hornet crews from VFA-14 knew that they might be prevented from bombing targets while aboard the *Lincoln* due to their jets being configured as tactical tankers, there was no shortage of volunteers to fly the two F/A-18Es from CVN-68 to the NAG. Unit CO Cdr Alton Ross told NAS Lemoore's base newspaper, *The Golden Eagle*;

'Every aviator in my ready room would have jumped at the opportunity to get to the fight early, but Lt Cdrs Hal Schmitt and Jason Norris were ultimately selected because of their overall strike credentials and their ability to fulfil any mission tasked in-theatre.'

As it transpired, both Schmitt and Norris saw combat in VFA-115 jets during their week aboard CVN-72 (*US Navy*)

VFA-41's F/A-18F BuNo 165878 was one of two Super Hornets sent by the unit to CVN-72. Seen here aboard the *Lincoln* soon after its arrival on 1 April 2003, the jet's underwing tanks were rapidly replaced with GBU-16 LGBs identical to the weapon seen in the foreground of this photograph. Several days later, one of the VFA-41 crews used an inert GBU-16 to good effect north of Baghdad, as CVW-11's Capt Chuck Wright explained to the author;

'Lts Tom Poulter and Tom Bodine were investigating a road intersection flyover when they spotted a multiple rocket launcher hidden beneath the road bridge, with dozens of cars driving by both on the bridge itself and on the road where the launcher was parked. They worked out that the only way to hit the target without causing massive collateral damage was to "safe" their GBU-16 and make it stupid. So they dropped the LGB without its fuse being armed, therefore turning it into a non-explosive 1000-lb solid concrete weapon. The bomb hit the launcher, sending dust and debris everywhere, followed seconds later by a huge explosion as the rockets cooked off. This showed that despite the crew doing everything they could to prevent large-scale destruction, they could not stop secondary explosions' (*US Navy*)

fire yet, and a definite attention getter. Our new targets were tanks and APCs in revetments. These were more difficult to find than bunkers, and required us to descend lower for positive target identification.

'As we worked hard to find the correct targets, we started seeing rocket and unguided missile fire – five or six salvoes – away to our north in the vicinity of Baghdad. Most of these appeared unable to reach our position, and we saw them explode in the distance. Our wingmen dropped their two remaining weapons first, and then we reset to the east for our attack run. As we set up, we picked up two more rocket/missile launches, this time from the east – our Tomcat's bombs had gotten someone else's attention. We took the appropriate evasive action, watched as the weapons pointed toward us and reached their apogee and then held our breath to see if they were guiding on us – luckily not, and both missiles exploded a couple of miles away. We continued with our attack, destroying a tank in a revetment, before controlling a section of British Harrier GR 7s that were targeting the same complex. Out of gas, we headed south for the NAG, and our third tanker.

'The next day we flew up to an area southeast of Baghdad to support Marine forces pushing north during our first Vul window. The difficulties of supporting troops in this conflict became readily apparent on this sortie, as they were taking fire from paramilitary forces using light trucks to pick at their flanks. For us, flying at above 10,000 ft, it was very difficult to distinguish between paramilitary forces and innocent civilians travelling along the roads. The conundrum was that the enemy was using suicide bomber tactics, which saw them trying to crash their explosive-laden vehicles into our Marines.

'Our solution was to strafe in front of cars and trucks that were closing on the Marine convoy with any speed – a sort of warning shot across the bow. If the vehicle continued to close to within one kilometre, then we would destroy it with a laser-guided weapon. Our flight completed three strafing runs on two separate trucks, and the drivers of both vehicles

pulled over to the side of the road after they saw the bullets impacting in front of them – they don't know how lucky they were! Luck was also on our side, as strafing required us to descend well below 5000 ft – right into the heart of the AAA and heat-seeking missile envelope.

'While setting up for our first strafing run to the west, my wingman and I had an unguided SAM explode several thousand feet above us. We immediately snapped our heads to the east and spotted the missile's contrail climbing out of a town some distance away – at times like these it's better to be lucky than good!

'Heading back into Iraq after tanking, dusk was falling, making visibility a definite cause for concern in respect to both target acquisition and threat avoidance. We returned to the 3rd Infantry Division and received a coordinate and frequency for our ground controller. Referencing our charts certainly got our adrenaline pumping, as we were headed to Baghdad International Airport! We checked in and got an update from the ground FAC – he was with forces south of the airport that were preparing to move north, and he wanted us to locate and destroy the artillery pieces that were firing on his troops.

'We spent a rather uncomfortable 40 minutes searching for targets. We knew that we were well within range of the city's missile defences, but amazingly no missiles were shot off in our direction, and we saw only sporadic AAA fire from the airport and its surrounding areas.

'In the twilight, with the thick oil fire smoke from Baghdad and the many fires burning in and around the airport, it was a surreal scene. The fairly heavy volume of surface fires only contributed to this scene, as the ground forces clashed with artillery and rocket launchers. We were unable to locate the camouflaged artillery pieces, but were able to target a dug-in troop emplacement guarding the southwest entrance to the airfield. We located their position on our FLIR and were cleared "hot" by the ground FAC, recording a good impact for both our weapons. Upon landing almost two hours later, we learned that the 3rd Infantry Division had pushed its way into the airport itself.

'On 4 April, with the ground forces advancing steadily on Baghdad, we headed northwest of the city to target a military complex housing

VFA-41's CAG jet escorts two Hornets from VFA-94 as they top off their tanks from a USAF KC-135R. 'Ace 100' was Capt Chuck Wright's assigned jet, the CAG of CVW-11 being a huge fan of the F/A-18E/F;

'The Super Hornet is far better than a seamless replacement for the Tomcat. A seamless replacement would be where you noticed no difference between the two types. Having operated F-14Ds with CVW-11 in OEF in 2002, I felt that it was much better to have Super Hornets in my wing in OIF in 2003. Indeed, I have not met a single Tomcat guy flying the Super Hornet now who has said he would rather go back to his old jet. The Super Hornet has better reliability, is more flexible in the ordnance it can carry and is easier to operate. The crew workload is far simpler in the Super Hornet in comparison with the Tomcat, for once you have learned the basics of "Hornetology" – essentially how to navigate through the mission computer, which you pick up during the first year of flying the jet – it's a "no brainer". Compared to the F-14, where just operating the Flight Management System (which managed the wing sweep) was a feat in itself, the Hornet is a dream. Indeed, the pilot-friendliness of "stuff" stashed in the cockpit of the Hornet is so much better than it is in the F-14. The HUD is better, the adaptability of NVGs is greater and the Joint Helmet-Mounted Cueing Sight is just out of this world' (*VFA-41*)

**Lt Cdrs Brian Garrison and Mark Weisgerber pose for a quick photograph on the deck of CVN-72 prior to flying their last combat sortie from the *Lincoln* on 6 April 2003. They flew back to CVN-68 later that night
(*Lt Cdr Mark Weisgerber*)**

A GBU-12-equipped F/A-18F of VFA-41 approaches Baghdad International Airport in late April 2003 (*VFA-41*)

artillery and tanks some ten miles north of our troops. Our ground controller provided coordinates and a target description based on some UAV imagery he had seen – this guy was quite good, and within minutes we had located the reveted artillery pieces and destroyed five sites. Unfortunately, there were no additional air assets available for us to control, as there were at least 15-20 additional targets within the complex. We stayed on-station until our fuel ran low, when we headed to the tanker.

'Upon our return, we were redirected to the southeast to support the Marines on another road reconnaissance mission. We provided cover for them as they went north, strafing a revetment suspected of firing on the convoy – we observed no fires, either surface-to-air or surface-to-surface.

'Lt Cdr Garrison and I conducted another night flight on the 5th, this time working west of the city, north of the airport and south of the city's main east-west highway. This was still a contested area on the ground, and we saw significant fighting on our NVGs.

'Our location was easy to mark visually, as there was a large ammo dump that had been targeted earlier in the day, and it would burn throughout the night – we could see weapons cooking off in all directions. This mission was a good lesson in joint warfighting, as the FAC had received targeting information from reconnaissance helicopters that had found some artillery pieces and a weapons cache complex.

'We split our flight, assigning the Tomcat to the artillery pieces in the south while we searched out the weapons bunkers to the north. Meanwhile, we had a flight of two F-15Es waiting to target whatever we located. After verifying we were on the right target (a laborious process at times, but very critical), we attacked two of the four bunkers and cleared the Strike Eagles to target the other two. Our Tomcat wingmen targeted

two artillery pieces to the south and provided laser guidance for a third bomb dropped by the Strike Eagles.

'We headed south for our mid-cycle gas and then flew north of Baghdad for our next assignment. By then our jet only had 20 mm ammunition left, while our F-14 still had an LGB. Continuing to work with the Army, we headed to an area that would become familiar over the next few days – Highway 1, leading north out of Baghdad to Tikrit.

'Our ground controller directed us to a location just off the highway, where intelligence indicated that a flatbed truck with a missile – a Free Rocket Over Ground (FROG) 7 – was hiding. Lacking a weapon to employ, we covered our wingmen from above while they looked for the target. After searching for some time, we had obviously drawn some attention to ourselves, for we started to see light AAA from the east as well from the city outskirts. After a couple of false targets, our F-14 wingmen located and successfully destroyed the FROG-7. We then climbed back up to 35,000 ft and headed south to the tanker, and eventually back to "Abe".

'6 April was our last day on *Lincoln*, and so as to facilitate our return to *Nimitz* that night, both VFA-41 jets launched on a morning mission as a flight of two Super Hornets. As we headed north off the tanker, we were directed to contact a ground controller called "Advance 15", and to "buster north", which meant that they wanted us to arrive as soon as possible. We accelerated north and checked in with "Advance 15".

'We quickly realised that our FAC was embedded with the Army units moving north of Baghdad to encircle the city – a fact that agreed with our pre-flight intelligence briefing. Weather and the missile threat from the city proper drove us west, so that we ingressed their position from the north, descending to about 11,000 ft, and below the overcast.

'Ace 104' returns to CVN-68 at the end of a post-OIF patrol over Iraq. The jet is armed with wingtip AIM-9Ms, a single AIM-120C and two Mk 20 Mod 3 Rockeye cluster bomb units. Post-war ops in the NAG were quite different to OIF missions, as Lt Tom Poulter explained in 1 August 2003 edition of *The Golden Eagle*;

'Our role now is morale suppression for the few remaining Iraqi militants, and providing support, when it is needed, for our guys on the ground. Believe it or not, just the presence of Navy fighters in the air really makes ground ops run more smoothly' (*US Navy*)

Home at last after nearly ten months on cruise, the pilots of VFA-115 prepare to meet their families at NAS Lemoore on 1 May 2003. Cdr Jeff Penfield is walking towards the camera immediately in front of the nose of VFA-115's CAG jet. He had nothing but praise for the Super Hornet following his unit's marathon cruise;

'I think that the F/A-18E/F enhances every mission that the standard Hornet does. Because of its fuel specification, you only need to fly the Super Hornet with one tank on its centreline, leaving a further six hardpoints available under the wings. The F/A-18C flies "double bubble" and they have only three hardpoints. The Super Hornet can bring more ordnance to the fight and stay at the fight longer. The jet's increased bring back capability ties right into that, allowing more contingency ordnance to be carried per mission.

'The jet's survivability is also greater thanks to the amount of ordnance it can carry. It can launch with four JDAM every time it goes flying, so a division of four jets can hit sixteen separate targets with precision. In *Desert Storm* you would have needed 16 Hornets to have hit this many targets, and VFA-115 could do it with four F/A-18Es in OIF. Right there, I have reduced the number of pilots that I have to send over the beach by 12. The F/A-18Cs in OIF could typically carry three JDAM over the beach, and over a period of time that extra bomb that my jets could carry further improved the survivability rate of my pilots, as I had to send less jets into Iraq to attack enemy targets' (*US Navy*)

'As we talked to "Advance", it became apparent that we would be supporting troops in contact with enemy forces – we could hear machine gun and small arms fire in the background as he described the current situation over the radio. They had proceeded south down Highway 1 to the outskirts of the city, and were now moving east on another road to secure a bridge over the Tigris River. Enemy forces were resisting on the near side of the river, and "Advance's" troops were taking fire.

'We continued to descend through the haze, setting up to strafe, since our 1000-lb bombs would simply cause too much collateral damage. Just like with our airport flight, this was a surreal scene. As our two aircraft proceeded south, flanking Highway 1 at 1000 ft, we saw multiple fires and burned out vehicles – remnants of the 3rd Infantry Division's opposed movement south. We located the major highway intersection that "Advance" had described, made a hard turn to the east and saw the friendly forces just east of the intersection. We then identified the bridge in question and reset to the north for our attack run(s). We executed two strafing passes in support of the ground forces, before returning to the tanker some 200 miles away. It is certainly easy to burn gas when you're low, fast and manoeuvring the aeroplane to avoid potential threats.

'Upon returning north 45 minutes later, the ground forces had successfully secured the bridge and were consolidating their hold on territory east of the river. We were directed to contact another ground controller just south who was moving east within the city itself. Our task was to search for several rocket launchers that had been firing earlier in the day. Our wingmen, working south of us, located the vehicles and proceeded to expend both of their LGBs while we provided high cover. Their second weapon scored a direct hit on the primary target, resulting in a tremendous explosion due to the explosives/fuel loaded in the vehicle. Out of time and gas, we headed home.

'After landing and debriefing, we had two hours to pack up and say goodbye before flying 200 miles south to *Nimitz* later that night. It had been a quick and action-packed week, and we had collected numerous "lessons learned" to be shared with the rest of CVW-11 prior to us starting combat ops from our own flight deck after only one day in-theatre.'

As with the A-7 Corsair II some three decades earlier, the Super Hornet had proven its worth in combat 'straight out of the box'. Destined to be in the vanguard of naval aviation for years to come, the jet had made a considerable contribution to Navy light strike's overall war effort in OIF.

APPENDICES

US NAVY NAG-BASED F/A-18 HORNETS AND SUPER HORNETS INVOLVED IN OIF

CVW-2 (USS *CONSTELLATION* (CV-64))

VFA-151 'VIGILANTES' (F/A-18C)

164716/300	164700/303	164713/306	164740/312
164703/301	164708/304	164739/307	164896/313
164897/302	164710/305	164719/310	164879/314

VFA-137 'KESTRELS' (F/A-18C)

164712/400	164704/403	164715/406	164707/411
164698/401	164709/404	164718/407	164736/412
164701/402	164693/405	164720/410	164895/414

CVW-5 (USS *KITTY HAWK* (CV-63))

VFA-27 'ROYAL MACES' (F/A-18C)

164045/200	164041/204	164016/207	164023/212
164002/202	163996/205	164003/210	164062/214
164010/203	164059/206	164008/211	164030/215

VFA-192 'WORLD FAMOUS GOLDEN DRAGONS' (F/A-18C)

164905/301	164971/305	164966/310	164903/313
164911/302	164958/306	164969/311	164979/314
164954/304	164962/307	164973/312	

VFA-195 'DAMBUSTERS' (F/A-18C)

164968/400	164977/403	164960/406	164904/411
164970/401	164980/404	164964/407	164907/414
164972/402	164974/405*	164900/410	

* shot down by Patriot missile on 2 April 2003

CVW-11 (USS *NIMITZ* (CVN-68))

VFA-41 'BLACK ACES' (F/A-18F)

165876/100	165880/104	165884/110	165888/114
165877/101	165881/105	165885/111	165894/115
165878/102*	165882/106	165886/112	
165879/103	165883/107*	165887/113	

* sent to CVN 72 on 30/3/03

VFA-14 'TOPHATTERS' (F/A-18E)

165861/200	165864/203	165867/206	165870/211
165862/201	165865/204	165868/207	165871/212*
165863/202*	165866/205	165869/210	165872/214

* sent to CVN 72 on 31/3/03

VFA-97 'WARHAWKS' (F/A-18A)

163098/300	162898/303	162860/306	163144/311
162900/301	162906/304	163092/307	163122/312
162897/302	163175/305	163106/310	163138/313

VFA-94 'MIGHTY SHRIKES' (F/A-18C)

164048/400	164047/403	163993/406	164052/411
163992/401	164067/404	164050/407	164042/412
163998/402	164055/405	163999/410	164021/413

CVW-14 (USS *ABRAHAM LINCOLN* (CVN-72))

VFA-115 'EAGLES' (F/A-18E)

165781/200	165784/203	165787/206	165790/211
165782/201	165785/204	165788/207	165791/212
165783/202	165786/205	165789/210	165792/214

VFA-113 'STINGERS' (F/A-18C)

164640/300	164658/303	164634/306	164242/311
164636/301	164638/304	164686/307	164220/312
164648/302	164641/305	164682/310	164257/313

VFA-25 'FIST OF THE FLEET' (F/A-18C)

164633/400	164664/403*	164654/406	164645/411
164635/401	164642/404	164660/407	164262/412
164637/402	164639/405	164676/410	164266/413

* participated in OSW but departed the runway at Pearce AFB, Western Australia, on 17/1/03 and was left behind until returned to US aboard CV-64 in 5/03

COLOUR PLATES

1
F/A-18C Hornet BuNo 164716 of VFA-151,
USS *Constellation* (CV-64), NAG, April 2003
VFA-151's CAG jet, this Lot XV machine has served exclusively with the 'Vigilantes' since December 1992. The aircraft is marked with the unit's 'Old Ugly' emblem (superimposed on the 'twin towers') on the inner surfaces of its vertical fins. It also features a full colour First Navy Jack on both sides of the fuselage and the dedication *In Memory of Ken Waldie* just aft of the cockpit. Waldie, who was a Naval Academy (Class of 1978) classmate of CVW-2 CAG Capt Mark Fox, died when American Airlines Flight 11 crashed into the World Trade Center on 11 September 2001.

2
F/A-18C Hornet BuNo 164703 of VFA-151,
USS *Constellation* (CV-64), NAG, April 2003
Delivered to the Navy in December 1992 and immediately allocated to VFA-151, this machine was one of twelve brand new night vision-capable Lot XV jets issued to the unit in 1992-93 as replacements for the 'Vigilantes'' veteran Lot VIII F/A-18As. CVW-2's jets weathered very quickly on cruise due to periodic fresh water shortages aboard CV-64. This effectively meant that deck crews were unable to wash their aircraft for extended periods – sometimes weeks on end. VFA-151 used a stylised dagger (part of its unit emblem) as a mission marking on its jets.

3
F/A-18C Hornet BuNo 164712 of VFA-137,
USS *Constellation* (CV-64), NAG, April 2003
'Falcon 400' was delivered to VFA-137 on 10 February 1993, the aircraft having the distinction of being the 10,000th TACAIR jet built by McDonnell Douglas. The only Hornet in the unit to boast colour markings, it was passed on to MAG-11's VMFA-232 at MCAS Miramar in late June 2003 as VFA-137 replaced its F/A-18Cs with new F/A-18Es.

4
F/A-18C Hornet BuNo 164709 of VFA-137,
USS *Constellation* (CV-64), NAG, April 2003
Taken on strength by VFA-137 in February 1993 when the unit replaced its Lot VIII F/A-18As with Lot XV F/A-18Cs, this aircraft was transferred to VMFA-232 in June 2003. Flown on several leaflet-dropping missions in OSW, 'Falcon 404' completed a further 19 combat sorties in OIF.

5
F/A-18C Hornet BuNo 164045 of VFA-27,
USS *Kitty Hawk* (CV-63), NAG, April 2003
Undoubtedly the most colourful Hornet to see combat in OIF, VFA-27's 'Mace 200' was the only colour jet from CVW-5's trio of F/A-18 squadrons to participate in CV-63's war deployment. VFA-192

left 'Dragon 300' at Atsugi and VFA-195 removed its 'bald eagle' and bold 'Chippy Ho' titling pre-cruise. BuNo 164045 was delivered to the Navy in December 1989 and initially issued to CVW-11's VFA-94. It was transferred to VFA-27 in early 1996 when the latter unit transitioned from Alpha to Charlie model Hornets prior to joining CVW-5 in Japan. The jet has been the 'Royal Maces'' CAG 'bird' since mid-1997.

6
F/A-18C Hornet BuNo 164979 of VFA-192,
USS *Kitty Hawk* (CV-63), NAG, April 2003
VFA-192 was the only light strike unit in CVW-5 to adorn its jets with mission markings, which took the form of nine LGB, eight JDAM, two Mk 82 and four JSOW silhouettes on 'Dragon 314'. This Lot XVII aircraft was delivered to the Navy in the summer of 1994, and was operated by Pacific Fleet Replacement Squadron VFA-125 from NAS Lemoore until passed on to VFA-192 at NAF Atsugi, Japan, in August 1998.

7
F/A-18C Hornet BuNo 164900 of VFA-195,
USS *Kitty Hawk* (CV-63), NAG, April 2003
'Chippy 410' was assigned to Lt Nathan White, who was killed by a Patriot missile on 2 April 2003 while flying 'Chippy 405' (BuNo 164974). A Lot XVI F/A-18C, BuNo 164900 was delivered to the Navy in late 1993 and issued to VFA-147. Thanks to the jet's '00' serial, it was a natural choice for CAG 'bird', and the Hornet remained in colour markings until it joined VFA-195 in August 1998 when CVW-9 and CVW-5 swapped F/A-18s.

8
F/A-18F Super Hornet BuNo 165877 of VFA-41,
USS *Nimitz* (CVN-68), April 2003
Both the CAG and CO jets of VFA-41 boasted near-identical full-colour markings, although the latter machine also featured the names of the four 'Black Aces' aircrew killed in a mid-air collision off the coast of California on 18 October 2002 on the outer surfaces of its twin tail fins.

9
F/A-18F Super Hornet BuNo 165878 of VFA-41,
USS *Abraham Lincoln* (CVN-72), NAG, April 2003
This jet was one of two F/A-18Fs forward-deployed to CVN-72 on 30 March 2003, BuNo 165878 being crewed by Lt Cdrs Mark Weisgerber and Brian Garrison. Appropriately, 'Ace 102' was also the jet which bore their names, and by the time the crew returned to CVN-68 on 6 April, it was adorned with 12 JDAM mission markings.

10
F/A-18E Super Hornet BuNo 165861 of VFA-14,
USS *Nimitz* (CVN-68) NAG, April 2003

One of the first F/A-18Es issued to VFA-14 in late 2001, this aircraft served as both a tanker and a bomber during CV-68's lengthy OIF deployment.

11
F/A-18E Super Hornet BuNo 165862 of VFA-14, USS *Nimitz* (CVN-68), NAG, April 2003
Again featuring full colour markings, VFA-14's CO jet had Tactical Paint Scheme grey vertical tail surfaces rather than glossy black. The 'Tophatters' got to deliver a number of LGBs, JDAM and laser Mavericks in the final days of OIF, the unit conducting numerous long-range missions to northern Baghdad and Tikrit.

12
F/A-18A Hornet BuNo 162906 of VFA-97, USS *Nimitz* (CVN-68), NAG, April 2003
VFA-97 flew the only carrier-based F/A-18As to see action in OIF, although the unit did not get to drop any ordnance prior to the bombing phase of the aerial campaign ending on 18 April. Borrowed from the Naval Strike Air Warfare Center (NSAWC) at NAS Fallon on the eve of CVW-11's deployment, 'Warhawk 304' stood out on the flightdeck thanks to its distinctive adversary paint scheme. A Lot VIII F/A-18A that was delivered to the Navy in October 1986, BuNo 162906 initially served with VFA-113 and was then passed on to VFA-27 in 1991. The jet remained with the 'Royal Maces' until early 1996, when the unit re-equipped with F/A-18Cs and BuNo 162906 was transferred to NSAWC.

13
F/A-18C Hornet BuNo 164048 of VFA-94, USS *Nimitz* (CVN-68), NAG, April 2003
Delivered to the Navy in July 1990, BuNo 164048 has served exclusively with VFA-94. During its 14 years of service with the 'Mighty Shrikes', the Hornet has flown numerous OSW patrols and seen combat in *Desert Fox*, OEF and OIF. It became VFA-94's 'Hobo 400' in early 2000.

14
F/A-18C Hornet BuNo 164633 of VFA-25, USS *Abraham Lincoln* (CVN-72), NAG, April 2003
Looking resplendent in its CAG colours, 'Fist 400' returned to NAS Lemoore on 1 May 2003 adorned with one JSOW and eight JDAM silhouettes. BuNo 164633 has served as the unit's CAG jet since its delivery to VFA-25 in October 1991.

15
F/A-18C Hornet BuNo 164635 of VFA-25, USS *Abraham Lincoln* (CVN-72), NAG, April 2003
'Fist 401' was marked with one HARM, two JSOW and 31 JDAM silhouettes – some of the latter represented LGB drops. Issued to VFA-113 in October 1991, BuNo 164635 transferred to VFA-25 in 1998, where it has always served as the CO jet.

16
F/A-18E Super Hornet BuNo 165781 of VFA-115, USS *Abraham Lincoln* (CVN-72), NAG, April 2003

VFA-115's CAG aircraft featured a scoreboard of 13 JDAM silhouettes, the jet expending this ordnance during OSW and the 'Shock and Awe' phase of OIF. It was then configured as a tanker until CVN-72 left the NAG on 7 April 2003. The aircraft also featured Station 54 Fire Department of New York-inspired artwork and a dedication to two of the senior firefighters killed in '9/11'.

17
F/A-18E Super Hornet BuNo 165782 of VFA-115, USS *Abraham Lincoln* (CVN-72), NAG, April 2003
The CO jet also boasted a mission scoreboard and nose art, as well as an 'In Memory of' dedication to fallen firefighters from '9/11' – VFA-115 forged strong links with the FDNY in the months after the attack on the World Trade Center. Like the squadron's CAG jet, BuNo 165782 featured colour markings, but not the black tail of BuNo 165781.

18
F/A-18C Hornet BuNo 164640 of VFA-113, USS *Abraham Lincoln* (CVN-72), NAG, April 2003
VFA-113 chose not to apply mission markings to its jets as the squadron boss felt that their application was an unnecessary burden on his already busy maintenance department. BuNo 164640 has been the unit's CAG jet since late 1991.

19
F/A-18C Hornet BuNo 164634 of VFA-113, USS *Abraham Lincoln* (CVN-72), NAG, April 2003
Lt Cdr Paul Olin was flying 'Sting 306' on the evening of 22 March 2003 when he fired the only SLAM-ER expended by a NAG-based Hornet in OIF. BuNo 164634 has served exclusively with VFA-113 since its delivery to the Navy in late 1991.

20
F/A-18C Hornet BuNo 165200 of VFA-82, USS *Enterprise* (CVN-65), NAG, January 2004
VFA-82 commenced patrols over Iraq in October 2003, although it almost certainly did not drop any bombs during its four months in the NAG. This aircraft has been the unit's CAG jet since it was delivered to VFA-82 in 1994. The Hornet was repainted in a garish bald eagle-inspired 'show bird' scheme in the final weeks of CVW-1's deployment aboard the *Enterprise*.

21
F/A-18C Hornet BuNo 163736 of VFA-86, USS *Enterprise* (CVN-65), NAG, January 2004
Operating the oldest F/A-18Cs in the fleet, VFA-86 performed myriad patrols in its veteran Lot X jets over Iraq in 2003-04. And unlike VFA-82, the unit got to deliver ordnance in anger when, on 9 January 2004, two Hornets each dropped a single 1000-lb JDAM apiece on a Fedayeen mortar position near the town of Balad, north of Baghdad. Delivered new to VMFAT-101 in February 1988, this jet subsequently served with VMFA-232 until passed onto VFA-86 in 2003. It wore OIF/OEF-inspired nose art during CVW-11s time in the NAG.

INDEX

References to illustrations are shown in **bold**. Colour Plates are shown with page and caption locators in brackets.